Asthma

THE FACTS

BY

DONALD J. LANE

Churchill Hospital, Oxford

WITH A CHAPTER BASED ON
PERSONAL EXPERIENCE BY

ANTHONY STORR

Warneford Hospital, Oxford

OXFORD UNIVERSITY PRESS

Oxford   New York   Toronto   Melbourne

OXFORD UNIVERSITY PRESS
Oxford   London   Glasgow
New York   Toronto   Melbourne
Nairobi   Dar es Salaam   Cape Town
Kuala Lumpur   Singapore   Hong Kong   Tokyo
Delhi   Bombay   Calcutta   Madras   Karachi

and associate companies in
Beirut   Berlin   Ibadan   Mexico City

British Library Cataloguing in Publication Data

Lane, D J

Asthma.—(Oxford medical publication).
1. Asthma
I. Title   II. Storr, Anthony   III. Series
616.2'3   RC591   79-40893
ISBN 0-19-261175-5
ISBN 0-19-520277-5 pbk.
UK ISBN 0-19-286021-6 pbk.

This printing (last digit):   9 8 7 6 5 4 3 2 1

Printed in the United States of America

Acknowledgements

No book is the unaided work of the person who appears as its author. This book is no exception. It is my pleasure therefore to acknowledge my indebtedness to the many patients whose experiences fill these pages, to researchers throughout the world who have provided the objective information on which many of the 'facts' are based, and to my colleagues here in Oxford whose comments and criticisms of the manuscript have led to the correction of many an error, and enabled me to clarify passages that my devious mind had made obscure. I would most like to thank personally Mrs Morag Maund who has devotedly and painstakingly typed and retyped the manuscript, the staff of Oxford University Press for cheerfully waiting for this manuscript to fight its way through to the top of my disorganized desk, and my wife who has tempered the excesses of my prose, ordered my syntax, and sacrificed many evenings of more pleasurable pursuits for the sake of this book.

Note to the reader

This book inevitably contains some technical terms. Each term is explained when it first appears in the text and the page number of this definition can be found in bold type in the index.

Contents

Introduction

ASTHMA AS A PERSONAL EXPERIENCE

I first developed asthma in early childhood, though I cannot remember exactly what age I was when I had my first attack. Neither of my parents was asthmatic; but of their four children three suffered from asthma and other allergic disorders. My elder brother developed asthma in adult life when practising as a doctor in Devonshire; whilst the elder of my two sisters had to be removed from school on account of it. Only the younger of my sisters escaped. My elder sister also had infantile eczema and an allergy to fish. Two of my three daughters have shown allergies of different kinds; one to plants, the other to horses; the former has hayfever, the latter has had an attack of asthma. The asthmatic tendency has been passed on to my sister's grandchildren. This is a rather characteristic family history, except that it is surprising that neither of my parents showed any allergic tendency. However, they were first cousins; so it seems likely that they were carrying recessive genes predisposing to the disease which were made manifest in their children.

During my childhood, asthma was not nearly so serious a problem as it has become much later in my life. I suffered much more from hayfever, which made me dread the summer. Asthma used to accompany hayfever, and also occurred in association with colds. I was a sickly child who became accustomed to illness at an early age; and if ever I caught a cold or influenza, it would 'go to my chest'. Once I had bronchopneumonia but whether this made me more or less liable to asthma I cannot say. My earliest recollection of having asthma is of myself sitting up in bed and leaning forward over a bed-table inhaling the smoke of 'Potter's Asthma Cure'. This was a powder containing stramonium (a drug which dilates the bronchi) which had to be ignited and which then emitted a smoke with a powerful and characteristic smell which comes back to me as I write. Potter's also made 'asthma cigarettes' containing the same powder. I have a vague recollection of smoking one of these and feeling very grown-up doing so; but I was not given them as often as the powder, which reminded me of one of those 'indoor fireworks' which one used to get out of Christmas crackers: a rather similar powder which also had to be ignited and which produced a long, snake-like shape when one set fire to it.

1

Introduction

It is also characteristic of the allergic 'diathesis', that I should have had at least one attack of giant urticaria, which is popularly known as 'nettle-rash' and that I should have reacted excessively to insect-bites. When I was a child it was possible to write on my skin with a fingernail as red wheals could be produced very easily. I am allergic to a number of different grass pollens, and still produce skin reactions to these when tested. I am also allergic to penicillin. Once, before I knew this, I was given an injection of penicillin. Within minutes my skin became distended with fluid, and my face swelled to such an extent that I could pick up sections of it as if was made of india-rubber. Fortunately this was in a hospital, and I was given an injection of adrenaline within a few minutes and quickly recovered. When I was thirteen I cut my head and developed a severe infection of the wound which rapidly led to infection of the bones of the skull and to a general septicaemia; that is, an infection severe enough for the bacteria causing it to be multiplying within the bloodstream. Today, this infection would have been cured within a few days by the administration of a suitable antibiotic; but, in 1933, even the sulphonamide group of drugs was not available, and I had to be given large doses of antistreptococcal serum to which, not unexpectedly, I had an allergic skin reaction.

My hayfever was treated by a long course of injections of 'Pollacine' which was developed in the laboratories of St Mary's Hospital as a way of desensitizing hayfever sufferers by giving them small but increasing doses of the pollens to which they were sensitive. I learned to give myself injections of this at the appropriate time of year, and persisted with them for several years. By the time I was about eighteen my hayfever was much less troublesome. I attributed this to the injections; but it is equally likely that the decline in severity was due to my having reached an age at which both hayfever and asthma often diminish or disappear, though why this happens is not known. Whatever the reason, I certainly lost both hayfever and asthma around that time, although I still became 'wheezy' if I caught a cold, and still developed irritation of the eyes during the summer even though I ceased to sneeze.

I cannot say that my childhood experience of asthma itself left any particular mark, for I did not have it nearly as severely as do many child asthmatics. On the other hand, it undoubtedly contributed to the picture which my parents and others had of me as 'delicate'. I was so often ill as a child that my parents decided that 'country air' would benefit me; and for this reason I was sent out of London to boarding

Introduction

school when I was eight years old. Like many other boys of my generation, I detested boarding school, and I am sure that the unhappiness I experienced there outweighed any possible benefit to my physical health. The effect of having asthma and other illnesses was to impair my physical confidence and to make me think of my body as a liability; a part of myself which I could not do without, but which was liable to let me down, and which was somehow inferior to those of other people. Freud rightly says that the ego is originally a body ego; that is, that our sense of identity is originally rooted in our physical being. I cannot remember a time when I liked my body or identified myself with it; it always seemed inefficient, or clumsy, or ailing. Physical confidence and confidence in other spheres go hand-in-hand; and my lack of physical confidence spread to include my abilities in general. Although I was for a time generally near the top of the class, by the time I was thirteen my performance deteriorated, and I did much less well throughout my school career than I should have. My impression is that many children who suffer a good deal of illness have the same experience. In my psychiatric work, I have generally managed to remember to enquire rather closely into my patient's history of physical illness in childhood, since I find that others have suffered in the same way as myself. Our adult psychological characteristics have roots in our childhood experience, and those who have a great deal of illness start with a disadvantage. However, a number of people react to this disadvantage as did Demosthenes to his stammer, or Franklin Roosevelt to his disablement by poliomyelitis. That is, they are driven to prove their worth by striving particularly hard to achieve something outstanding. Alfred Adler, who was originally an associate of Freud, but who parted from him to found his own school of 'Individual Psychology' laid emphasis upon how a particular physical weakness or 'organ inferiority', as he named it, could spur a person on to compensate or overcompensate, and thus achieve more than average in spite of a disability.

By the time I went to Cambridge—in 1939—my health had improved, although I still became wheezy if I caught a cold. During my time at Westminster Hospital as a medical student I had an operation on my nose to remove a deflected nasal septum, the barrier down the middle of one's nose which separates the nostrils, and which is sometimes bent to one side or the other. I suspect that the fact that my nose so often became blocked was more due to allergic swelling of the mucous membrane than to the effects of a deflected septum; but the operation did something to relieve what had been a chronic problem.

3

Introduction

From 1939–69, however, I was almost free of asthma, although I continued to become wheezy to a very slight degree if I caught a cold, and always had a supply of ephedrine on hand to combat this. In 1969 asthma returned. Two factors may have contributed to this. First, I had another operation on my nose. By the end of 1968 I had lost my sense of smell altogether. Although this can in some circumstances be an advantage, the disadvantages outweigh the gains. One's sense of taste depends much more upon one's sense of smell than most people realize —one's actual taste buds only distinguish sweet, sour, salt, and bitter— and I could no longer enjoy food or drink in the way that I had done previously. The operation, known as an ethmoidectomy, cleared my nose of polyps, that is allergic swellings of the mucous lining of the nose, which were preventing odours from reaching my olfactory nerve, and my sense of smell was restored, at any rate partially. I later discovered that some authorities advise asthmatics against having nasal surgery unless it is absolutely essential on the grounds that it may make their asthma worse. However, there were no immediate effects from the operation, which was performed in the spring of 1969, and I cannot prove, though I strongly suspect, that it contributed to the return of asthma later that year.

The other factor which may have played its part was a period of stress which occurred in July and August of the same year. In 1968 a book of mine called *Human Aggression* was published and achieved a modest success. On the strength of this I was invited to Harvard to give a course of lectures and seminars in their summer school. I had never taught undergraduates before, though of course I had taught doctors, nurses, social workers, and others in the course of my various appointments as a psychiatrist. Nor had I ever been to America. I remember arriving in Boston in intense heat—the temperature was in the nineties—which was accompanied by equally intense humidity. I took a taxi to the apartment I was renting from an art historian which was close to Harvard Yard. The apartment had been shut up for the past three weeks, with all the curtains drawn, and the temperature inside must have been about 130° Fahrenheit. I remember thinking that if this was what America was like I would have to go home. However, I succeeded in settling in and giving my two courses. One, which I much enjoyed, was to a small class of about twelve highly intelligent graduates on 'Creativity'. The other, which I dreaded, was to a class of about eighty undergraduates, on 'Aggression'. The lectures cannot have been a disaster, since I have been asked back to Harvard; but I cannot flatter myself that they were very good and I certainly

4

Introduction

felt tense and anxious during a good deal of the time I was in Harvard, although I also enjoyed a great deal of my stay, and made many new friends.

On my return, I went for a brief holiday to the Lake District. A third factor which may have contributed to the return of the asthma was that this particular house was ill-cared for and extremely dusty. However that may be, I developed a cough and wheeziness, and, to my horror, found that I could no longer walk as far as I had been accustomed to. Although never particularly robust, I had at least been able to walk; and, on my holiday in the previous year, had been able to walk twenty miles or more in a day in the mountains of Czechoslovakia.

At first, I did not believe that I had asthma, thinking that my cough and wheeziness was the result of bronchitis. But it soon became obvious that infection was not the prime cause, and I had to learn to accept the fact that, after thirty years of almost complete freedom from the disease, I was once again 'an asthmatic'.

As is common enough, my symptoms fluctuated in severity during that autumn. Then, in December 1969, I had a really bad attack. It so happened that, through no fault of his, my general practitioner could not be reached for a considerable time. I was in bed, panting away, wholly absorbed in the question of how I could get enough air into my lungs, although by this time my breathing was out of voluntary control and had become purely automatic. I began to realize that this attack was not only the worst attack of asthma which I had ever had myself, it was the worst attack that I had ever seen in anybody. Although I had been practising psychiatry for many years, I had, of course, treated asthmatics when I was a medical student and a house physician, and was familiar with attacks severe enough to warrant the patient's admission to hospital. As time went on, and the attack showed no signs of subsiding, I suddenly realized that I was in danger. I remember thinking to myself, 'If this goes on much longer, I might die'. At this point, I had a curious experience which has been reported before in those who have been close to death but lived to recount their story. I had what has been called an 'out-of-body experience'. That is, I became, as it were, detached from my own body, and almost seemed to be looking down on my heaving, panting frame from some point above it. At the same time, my anxiety and fear of dying was replaced by a sense of calm. I remember thinking, 'It might go either way. I wonder which way it will go. Perhaps this is the end of my life'. I did not find myself reviewing the events of my life, although I did think with regret that those dependent on me might find it more difficult to manage without me.

5

Introduction

When my doctor finally arrived, he was clearly more anxious than I was myself. Fortunately, he carried oxygen in his car, and I was soon finding some partial relief by breathing it. He also gave me an injection of cortisone, and telephoned to the chest specialist whom I had consulted to enquire whether there was anything else he could do. Since he was an extremely experienced and conscientious doctor, there was, of course nothing else that the chest physician could suggest. I owe my friend Dr John Horder my life, and take this opportunity of thanking him, not only for saving me on this occasion, but for innumerable instances of devoted care over many years.

My 'out-of-body' experience is what psychiatrists call a 'schizoid' phenomenon. That is, it is an instance of a wider variety of phenomena which have in common the fact that, for the time, the person concerned is detached from the emotion which he would normally be expected to be feeling concurrently. If we are faced with something which is deeply painful or frightening, a protective mechanism comes into operation which prevents us being overwhelmed by grief or fear. Thus, a person who has been bereaved may, for a week or two, say that he feels numb or apathetic, and be unable to weep or show other signs of grief. A similar numbness often affects those who have been exposed to disasters like earthquakes. Sometimes those who have been through very disturbing experiences suffer from various symptoms like depression, anxiety, insomnia, and irritability which persist until they have been able to 'relive' the experience, and express the emotion connected with it which they were unable to express at the time; a phenomenon to which psychiatrists who treated battle casualties during the last war became accustomed. More often, the sufferer gradually works through his disturbing experience by repeatedly telling his friends about it until it seems to lose its emotional charge.

Although, like many asthmatics, I have from time to time had dreams of being drowned or stifled, I was not left with any severe after-effects from my experience of nearly dying, though it did leave me with a vivid realization that severe asthma is something to be taken seriously. It still seems to be a popular belief that people never die of asthma. In fact, some 1000 people in Great Britain die of it every year.

I have subsequently had a number of attacks of asthma, but only one has been as bad, or nearly as bad as this first really severe attack. This occurred whilst I was on holiday in Wales. My wife and I owned a cottage in a rather remote part of Wales on the borders of Snowdonia. We were there together when I developed severe asthma one evening which did not respond to treatment. My wife tried to summon help, but the telephone was out of order. By the time this was discovered, I was so bad that she did not like to leave me, nor did I wish her to do so. We decided together that for her to fetch a doctor from the village was out of the question; and it also became obvious that I could not be driven to hospital as I was too ill to walk to the car, and she obviously could not carry me unaided. We therefore decided to stay together. Fortunately, when I felt that any breath might be my last, the spasm suddenly eased, and I started to recover. Experiences like this have taught me that it is wise to take precautions in advance, such as making sure that the telephone is working, and making contact with local medical facilities.

Since asthma returned in 1969 I have been what is known as a severe chronic asthmatic. Although miracles sometimes happen, in this disease more than in others, I have no sustained hope of getting rid of it before my death. However, with the help of my doctors, Godfrey Fowler and Donald Lane, I have sufficiently mastered the disease for it to have become not entirely unreasonable to think that I might live long enough to die of something else. I now have much less time off work than I did when I first began to get bad attacks; although I may have to be away for a day or two when a bad attack first starts. I was admitted to hospital twice in the early part of 1976; but since then I have not been in hospital, which I attribute to my having learned something more about how to prevent attacks becoming out of hand. I therefore turn from a consideration of my own history to the problem of how to deal with asthma as a patient, in the hope that my experience may be of some use to others.

It has taken me a long time to learn how to cope with asthma at all effectively in spite of my medical training. One of the curious features of the disease, which others have noticed and commented upon, is a kind of false optimism between attacks. When asthma returns, it is natural enough to be somewhat depressed. Indeed, some observers believe that attacks of asthma are usually anticipated or accompanied by quite marked depression. I have not been sure that depression precedes an attack in my case, but I am sure that, once an attack is past, I am unrealistically euphoric and disposed to think that I may never have another. This extends to believing that, when asthma does start, it will not be very bad 'this time', and that I need not, therefore, take all the rather distasteful steps which are necessary to control it. This has meant that, in the past, I was reluctant to summon medical help even when the attack was obviously severe. I used to boast that I never allowed anyone to call the doctor until I was so breathless that I could no longer

Introduction

speak, but had to communicate in writing. I do not leave things so long today. A recent investigation in the Cardiff region showed that fatal attacks were typically short, lasting less than 30 minutes in 23 per cent and less than two hours in 25 per cent. It was also demonstrated that both patient and doctor were prone to underestimate the severity of the attack. I do not want to alarm my fellow sufferers, many of whom, although asthmatic, may never have had in the past or have in the future an attack which threatens life: but I do want to attack the conspiracy, to which asthma sufferers themselves contribute, which alleges that 'no-one ever dies of asthma', and which contributes to unnecessary deaths by not taking severe attacks seriously. In Edinburgh, asthmatics who have previously been in hospital with severe asthma are encouraged to admit themselves to hospital without the need of medical referral. This probably saves a number of lives as, although there is no evidence from the Cardiff figures that there was any undue delay in the general practitioners getting to their asthmatic patients, it clearly saves time if the patient himself can initiate admission to hospital when necessary.

This brings me to another, most important aspect of coping with severe asthma. One is naturally reluctant to summon medical help unnecessarily, or to enter hospital unless it is absolutely essential, so that one is predisposed to treat severe attacks of asthma less seriously than is warranted. An interesting book on psychological factors in asthma by Aaron Lask, *Asthma: Attitude and Milieu* (Tavistock, 1966), one of the many general practitioners trained in psychotherapy by the psycho-analyst Michael Balint, finds that the most severe asthmatics share an attitude of independence and reluctance to seek help. When Dr Lask and a group of his fellow practitioners started to investigate their population of asthmatics, they expected to find that a great many of them were demanding, using their illness as an excuse for getting attention and summoning the doctor when it was not necessary. In fact, though such patients existed, they formed only 15 per cent of the adult asthmatics in the practices investigated. Dr Lask found that most adult asthmatics managed their illness alone, and were reluctant to confide or to ask for help. I share this attitude. Moreover, however experienced one may be, it is extremely difficult to predict how severe any given attack is going to become. Sometimes, one may be severely breathless and noisily wheezy, and the attack will subside without progressing to anything alarming. At other times, an apparently less threatening attack will rapidly become severe. What is needed is an objective way of assessing the probable severity of an attack.

I have found that the use of a peak flow meter goes a long way to

Introduction

meeting this need. This is a device for measuring the rate at which one can force air out of one's lungs when one takes as deep a breath as one can, and then blows it out as fast as possible. If one blows into a peak flow meter, the needle records one's performance in litres per minute. As every asthmatic knows, breathing out is more difficult than breathing in; and the more the bronchi are obstructed by spasm and swelling, the more difficult it is to force air out of the lungs. Therefore, peak flow is a fairly objective measure of the degree of obstruction of the bronchi, and thus is a reliable indicator of the severity of the asthma. Since readings may vary slightly, it is advisable to take the best of three readings on any one occasion.

I have found that a great reduction in my peak flow often occurs *before* my asthmatic symptoms have become severe. In fact, I often refer to my peak flow meter as my early warning system. I have been in the habit of recording peak flow at the same time each morning and evening for a number of years, with the result that, by using appropriate drugs, I have been able to catch attacks at an early stage and prevent them from becoming too severe.

It is interesting to speculate as to why peak flow should be a better indicator of bronchial obstruction than one's own awareness of breathlessness. I think the answer is that, unless one has to climb stairs or run, one can suffer quite a large diminution in one's respiratory efficiency without being fully aware of how great that reduction is. If one is in good health, one does not realize what an enormous difference there is in one's requirements of oxygen when walking on the flat as compared with walking up stairs or running. Asthmatics soon become particularly aware of this discrepancy but, even so, can be deceived. When lying in bed or sitting still little oxygen is needed, and it is easy to be misled as to how difficult it may be to get more oxygen when that is required. I am sure I am not alone amongst asthmatics in having often woken in the morning with a conviction that an attack of asthma has almost subsided only to find that, when I get out of bed to empty my bladder, I am far more breathless than I had supposed. A peak flow meter will reveal the true state of affairs.

In my own case, as the Figure overleaf demonstrates, a sudden drop in peak flow is a valuable warning sign, in exactly the same way as a drop in barometric pressure is a warning sign of rain to come.

The marked difference between readings in the early morning and readings in the early evening is not fully understood. If one is taking drugs for asthma, and takes the morning reading before having any medicines, as I do, the swing may be partly accounted for by the fact

9

Introduction

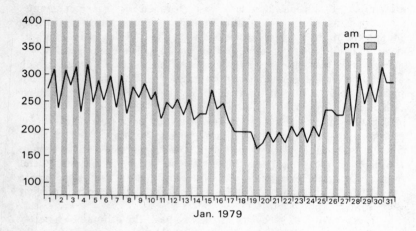

am ☐
pm ▨

Jan. 1979

that the overnight gap between doses of medicine is the longest in the twenty-four hour period. Whatever the reason, my own peak flow, in between attacks of asthma, varies between 200 litres per minute in the morning and 300 litres per minute (or more if I am in particularly good form) in the evening. If the reading drops below about 140 litres I know I am in for trouble, and I am inclined to summon, or at least alert, my doctor. If it drops further, to about 120 or less, I am virtually immobilized; completely so if the reading is only 100. These figures are not to be taken as applying to anyone else; though we do have a clear idea of what is 'normal' in the average adult. It is simply to demonstrate that one's own, extremely shaky, unreliable subjective judgement can be reinforced by something much more objective which can provide a useful indication of what steps ought to be taken to both oneself and one's doctor.

I am quite sure that peak flow meters ought to be issued to all severe asthmatics. They are simple to use: and most patients can easily be taught to record morning and evening readings as I do.

From my own experience, and from what others tell me, I am certain that prevention in asthma is all-important. There is some curious

10

mechanism, which we do not fully understand, which causes asthma to grow by what it feeds on. Although attacks cannot wholly be prevented, they can, to some extent, be anticipated; and the sooner remedial measures are begun, the less likely is the attack to become a bad one. Because asthmatics, as I have already mentioned, tend to be unrealistically optimistic, they often postpone taking steps to prevent an attack becoming severe, since they continue to hope that it will not become so. Asthmatics must learn to become self-medicators; to agree with their doctors what drugs are suitable in their particular circumstances, and to be familiar with the minimum and maximum effective doses of each. They will then be in a position to increase each drug to its permitted maximum whenever an attack threatens, reducing the dose if the attack passes off.

Severe attacks of asthma are alarming; and even if the thought of death itself is not necessarily threatening, inability to get enough air in and out of one's lungs is in itself a horrible, frightening experience, which provokes considerable anxiety. So much is this the case, that, in various parts of the world, mechanical interference with respiration is a well-known method of torture. In many prisons, those who are being interrogated have their heads plunged under water, which is often full of excreta, until they are nearly drowning. Another well-tried technique is to lie the victim down and pile slabs of stone on to his chest until it becomes more and more difficult for him to breathe at all. I can imagine exactly what such a prisoner feels. However, anxiety actually increases one's difficulty in breathing, and one can learn to control anxiety to some extent. Anxiety makes one breathe even more rapidly and shallowly than one needs; whereas exactly the opposite is required during a bad attack of asthma. Therefore, one must school oneself to breathe as deeply and slowly as is possible even whilst in the throes of an attack. One difficulty in doing this is that deeper breathing may make one cough; and coughing when the attack is at its height, makes one even more breathless. In a very severe attack, oxygen is often valuable. It is possible for doctors to prescribe oxygen under the NHS. I myself have a cylinder in my bedroom. Although I seldom need to use it, it is a comforting presence, and has in fact been invaluable on more than one occasion.

The anxiety which accompanies very great difficulty in breathing is also relieved to some extent by the presence of a loved one, and the touch of a loving hand. I feel no shame at all in recording that, when I have been desperately breathless, being able to grasp my wife's hand is enormously comforting.

Introduction

When one is very breathless, to be able to sit up comfortably is very important. No asthmatic needs telling that his breathing is easier when he is sitting up than lying down; and most asthmatics will have their own arrangements of pillows which suit them. However, it is worth mentioning that it is easy to make a special bed-rest modelled on those huge cushions filled with plastic particles which were fashionable as substitutes for chairs some years ago. A smaller version of these has the advantage that, whilst it gives good support, it is also softer and more malleable than the ordinary bed-rest. However, bed itself is not a comfortable place for asthmatics, since it is easier still to breathe if one's legs are hanging down. So sitting in a suitable chair, provided one can be kept warm, is still more comfortable. The idea that one must be 'in bed' if very ill is difficult to dispel; but I think that it is easier to manage asthma oneself if one is sitting up in an armchair.

During a bad attack of asthma one's appetite usually disappears entirely. Moreover, eating generally makes one's breathlessness worse. However, one has to try and eat something, at least when the attack is beginning to subside, and my own experience has led me to believe that little and often is far better than having a large meal. It is extremely important, however bad one is, to drink large quantities of fluid; and it will be found that to do so does not increase, and may diminish, the severity of the symptoms. I find that lime juice or lemon barley water encourages me to drink more than I would if I confined myself to water which, in cities in Great Britain, is often so heavily chlorinated as to taste extremely unpleasant. The reason that one ought to drink as much fluid as possible during asthma is that one becomes dehydrated during a bad attack. There is some evidence that the extreme stickiness of the sputum, which constitutes one of the most tiresome features of asthma, is reduced if one imbibes enough fluid.

Sleep is always a problem during the course of a bad attack of asthma. It is always disturbed, and one may only be able to doze intermittently throughout the night. It is important not to take any kind of sleeping pill, since nearly all such medicines tend to depress respiration still further. I have found, however, that a very small quantity of whisky enables me to get some sleep without having any adverse effect that I can detect.

If one has a sleeping partner, problems may arise. On the one hand, a bad attack of asthma may demand immediate help; unscrewing the nut on the oxygen cylinder, for instance; or telephoning the doctor if the attack gets worse. On the other, knowing that one is keeping one's partner awake increases one's own anxiety and distress. In the house I live

Introduction

in, we have solved the problem by my wife being able to sleep in a bedroom immediately opposite to the one we usually share. We both leave our doors slightly ajar; and I have a small handbell which I can ring if things get desperate. This works very well, as I prefer to be alone when having asthma in order to be free to cough, move in bed, put the light on and so on without disturbing anyone else.

It is also a great advantage if the room in which one sleeps is on the same level as a lavatory. I share the dislike of bedpans and bottles which most patients have; and if I can manage to totter to a lavatory during even a bad attack of asthma, I do so.

When a bad attack of asthma subsides, it is important to take things slowly and easily. Objective tests show that one's blood gases and metabolism take time to get back to normal; and a bad attack leaves one exhausted for a while.

The main problem of the aftermath, at any rate in my case, is to get rid of the accumulated sticky sputum which is such a feature of asthma, and which, in fatal cases, is the cause of death by plugging the smaller air passages. I think it is important to clear one's lungs of this as fast as possible: for my private, unsubstantiated belief is that the more mucus which remains in the bronchial tree, the more does it act as an irritant provoking both the production of still more mucus, and also bronchoconstriction. During a bad attack of asthma, coughing may have to be suppressed, since it sometimes increases breathlessness to an intolerable degree. When the attack is subsiding, I find that coughing is often far less helpful in getting rid of sputum than I would like it to be. I think this is because coughing tends to constrict the bronchi still further, which makes it impossible for the sputum to be expelled. I have found it useful to breathe out against slight resistance: that is, by pursing one's lips as if one was going to whistle and then breathing out in a slow and determined fashion. This technique helps to bring up sputum to the point at which it can gently be coughed up without difficulty. Another valuable way of hurrying mucus up the bronchial tree is to blow one's nose gently. It is important to avoid violent coughing as much as possible since this is not only exhausting, but also may damage one's lungs.

When physiotherapy is available, this is often helpful in speeding up the process of clearing one's chest of accumulated secretion. Physiotherapists often use a 'Bird' respirator which blows humidified oxygen into one's lungs. This can help one to clear out the loosened sputum by a combination of techniques of 'assisted respiration' and 'postural drainage'. (See Plate VII.)

13

Introduction

Although, as a medical student, I was taught that expectorant drugs were largely useless, research has shown that some drugs do accelerate the passage of mucus up the bronchial tree. I use a preparation containing guiaphenesin.

I am also a believer in the old-fashioned remedy of 'inhaling'. It probably does not matter whether one uses Friar's Balsam or one of the modern, proprietary capsules which have largely replaced it, since it is likely to be the steam, rather than whatever is added to it which is helpful. However, I have found that sticking one's head over a jug of boiling water with some reasonably pleasant-smelling medicament in it does seem to loosen sputum and make it easier to expel. The smell of eucalyptus is difficult to get rid of; and so I use a special jug for inhaling. Plastic jugs which withstand boiling water are now available, and seem very suitable. So much for dealing with the attack.

In between attacks I try to be a 'good patient' and obey my doctors' instructions. That is, I take the drugs which they tell me to take, although it is a nuisance never to be able to travel anywhere without carrying two different aerosols and a variety of tablets. Although I am not taking oral steroids all the time, I do have to take large doses when an attack starts; and, by the time I have reduced the dose to nil, I generally have only a week or two before the next attack occurs. I dislike having to take steroids because, like many other people, I dislike being dependent on drugs which interfere with the roots of my emotional being and also alter my facial appearance. One's hormonal system, unlike one's stomach or kidneys, is intimately connected with one's sense of self and one's emotional responsiveness. I haven't suffered severely from the emotional disturbances which are described in some patients who have to take steroids, apart from one short-lived attack of depression: but I confess to a feeling of unease that these powerful drugs may not only relieve asthma but alter my personality.

Although my capacity for physical exercise is now impaired, I do try to take some, and also try not to put on weight; a tendency which is enhanced by steroids. Large meals tend to make me wheezy, and so I usually avoid them. Some forms of alcohol seem to provoke asthma; but whisky seems the least provoking of alcoholic drinks, and I drink this in preference to other forms of alcohol.

As a psychiatrist, I shall be expected to say something about psychological factors in asthma, which is often labelled a 'psychosomatic' disease. When I was a medical student, it was fashionable to suppose that asthma, duodenal ulcer, ulcerative colitis, hypertension and a few other diseases were primarily the result of emotional conflicts. In

14

Introduction

Chicago, the psychoanalysts Alexander and French thought that they had pinpointed the psychological cause of asthma, amongst other diseases. They believed that asthma took origin from a particular conflict, starting in childhood, which consisted of a deep dependence upon the mother or mother-substitute combined with a fear of becoming estranged from her by somehow offending her. In *Psychoanalytic therapy* they quote a case of a young man whose asthma was relieved by psychotherapy when he came to realize that his dependence upon his stepmother was complicated by sexual desires toward her. In other cases, it was supposed that the child had aggressive feelings toward his mother which he dared not express for fear of losing her support. There are two difficulties about this kind of explanation. One is that the number of cases described is minute, so that there is really no evidence that the explanation invoked fits more than a tiny minority. The other is that, especially in the case of psychosomatic disorders, the psychopathology which is postulated is generally concerned with conflicts and impulses which are universal. What human being, in childhood, has not had conflicts between dependence and independence? Which of us have not felt aggressive towards those upon whom we are dependent? The hope that any given psychosomatic disorder has a specific emotional conflict at the root of it has not been fulfilled. Indeed, many of us have given up using the term 'psychosomatic' in the belief that it is a cloak for ignorance rather than a description of any value. This is not to say that stress is incapable of precipitating asthma, or of making it worse once it is established. In my career as a psychiatrist I remember one case of asthma, though only one, in which I felt certain that stress had played the major part in initiating the disease. This was the case of a lady who had her first attack of asthma in middle age, and who went on to become a severe asthmatic. Before the asthma started she had been subjected to considerable stress in that her husband had developed a premature form of senility due to brain disease (presenile dementia). Since he was incapable of earning, his wife had had to take on the responsibility of going out to work for the first time in her life in order to meet the rather heavy financial commitments which the family had shouldered. That her asthma was directly connected with her husband's collapse was demonstrated by her dream that she was tightly wrapped in a carpet whilst he sat on her chest, making it almost impossible for her to breathe. Such cases are, however, rare; and I do not think that stress of this kind is often a sufficient, although it may be a subsidiary factor, in provoking asthma.

Various investigations have been undertaken in the hope of discovering

Introduction

an asthmatic personality; but there is little evidence that such a thing exists. Some asthmatics are neurotic; others are not; and when asthmatics do show neurotic traits, it is hard to decide whether these traits are a cause or a result of the disorder. There is, however, some consensus of opinion that asthmatics are overcontrolled and tend to bottle up their emotions. Dr Lask and his colleagues, whose work I referred to earlier, found that the majority of asthmatics were reluctant to ask for help, but that the minority who made many demands upon their doctors tended to have attacks of asthma which were less severe. This finding might be interpreted as evidence that asthmatics are essentially rather dependent people but are reluctant to admit or to give in to this aspect of their personalities. This interpretation is supported by one study which found that in Maryland, asthma was more commonly found in boys from middle-class families in which particular emphasis is laid upon achievement and independence. In dealing with my own asthma I have learned that to try to maintain too stiff an upper lip is a mistake, in that it is better to seek help early rather than later.

However, there is no doubt that emotional stress has an effect upon asthma once it is established, although it is difficult to predict whether emotional arousal will make asthma worse or better. The physician Sir Arthur Hurst once had an attack of asthma whilst driving. He fumbled a gear change and found himself speeding down a hill in neutral with the car out of control. By the time he had reached the bottom of the hill his asthma had disappeared. Hurst supposed that his anxiety had caused his adrenal glands to produce more adrenaline, which thus relieved his asthma; but anxiety does not invariably have this effect. I can recall two instances in my own case in which anxiety made asthma worse. One was when I thought that a hotel had overcharged me, and that I should have to dispute the bill, a thing which I very much dislike having to do. The other was when I was in charge of my two-year-old grandson when he slipped and cut his head. As soon as I had taken him in to his mother and made sure that he was not badly injured my wheeziness subsided. The fact that asthma can be made worse or relieved by emotional arousal does not imply that the cause of asthma is primarily emotional. It is hard to think of any physical condition which is not influenced by the patient's emotional state, from headache to rheumatoid arthritis. However, if stress does play a part in inducing asthma, I suggest that our failure to have discovered a more clearcut relationship between supposed cause and effect may be due to the fact that stress has effects which may not be manifested for years after the event. We know that people who have been in concentration camps

16

Introduction

suffer both in physical and mental health for years afterwards; probably for the rest of their lives. But we do not yet know in detail how the effects of stress are mediated. The endocrine system, particularly, is enormously complicated; and, although advances in understanding are made every year, we are still ignorant about many features of its functioning. I am quite prepared to believe that my personality and that of other asthmatics is related to peculiarities in my physical constitution; more particularly to peculiarities in the endocrine system and those physiological functions which are concerned with defence against disease. But I think that, in our present state of ignorance, it is premature to make any generalizations about personality characteristics or neurotic traits in any so-called psychosomatic disease, including asthma.

I will not pretend that asthma is anything but a liability which I would much rather be without. However, whenever I am inclined to be sorry for myself, I think of those who have to cope with chronic illnesses which are far, far worse, like multiple sclerosis. Thanks to a great deal of expert, devoted help from my colleagues, I have learned to cope and to live with asthma; and I look forward to the day when the underlying cause of this common disease will be better understood than it is today.

The following chapters depict the facts about asthma as they are known today. Greater understanding has, in my case, helped me to live with asthma and overcome many of the problems associated with it. I hope that others may be able to benefit as I have.

1

What is asthma?

ASTHMA is a condition which is easy to recognize, yet difficult to define. There can be few who have not seen the attacks of wheezy laboured breathing that are the hallmark of asthma. It commonly afflicts the young, though they frequently grow out of it. It may return or occur for the first time in middle life. Death from asthma is uncommon, but not so infrequent that either doctors or patients can be complacent.

The difficulty in precise definition lies in the fact that other conditions besides asthma can cause wheezy breathing. It is the variable nature of the wheezing that will classify the condition as asthma rather than something else. Defining a degree of variability that makes wheezing episodic rather than continuous is entirely arbitrary. Since arbitrary decisions lead to contention it is not perhaps surprising that when a group of experts sat down to *define* asthma in 1972 they came to the conclusion that on the evidence currently available they could not do so. Yet each freely admitted to the others, that they could readily *recognize* asthma when they saw it.

These perplexities can perhaps be better understood by taking an historical perspective. The word asthma is Greek. It meant panting and was one of the words coined to describe shortness of breath. Laboured and difficult breathing was called dyspnoea, 'dys', meaning difficult, and '-pnoea' meaning breathing. Breathing difficulties when lying flat were orthopnoea; 'ortho', meaning straight or flat. These two words are still in use and so, of course, is asthma. From the very beginning it signified a breathing difficulty that, whilst alarming when it happened, came only sporadically.

Some of the most eloquent descriptions of asthma come from Aretaeus the Cappadocian in the second century AD. 'The lungs suffer and the parts which assist respiration sympathize with them'. He wrote of the rapid noisy breathing of the asthmatic and of the anxiety and fear it

What is asthma?

induced. 'They eagerly go into the open air, since no house sufficeth for their respiration.'

The accurate clinical observations of Aretaeus were lost for over a millenium whilst medicine lay under the influence of Galen. Born at Pergamon in Asia Minor in AD 131, Galen constructed a formidable corpus of medical theory and practice. He contributed significantly to understanding of the nervous system, but he completely misunderstood the function of the lungs and heart. For Galen the heart was a fire warming the body. Breathing brought in fresh air to cool its fiery furnace and instil 'pneuma', the vital spirit, into the blood. Exhaled breath, warmed by its encounter with the heart's heat, carried away impurities. The invigorated blood was thought to ebb and flow through the tissues. Medicine had to wait fifteen centuries for Harvey to demonstrate its circulation.

Galen had little of worth to offer on asthma. The Arabian physician Rhazes remarked, 'Galen said that many cure asthma with owl's blood given in wine. I say that owl's blood is not to be given, for I have seen it administered and it was useless.' Two sparks of insight briefly lighten these dark Galenic ages. One was from Paulus Aegimetri. In the seventh century AD he supposed that 'thick and viscid humours' were responsible for blocking the passage of air into the lungs. Considering the strange misconceptions held at the time about the anatomy of the lungs, this view is surprisingly in keeping with modern findings.

Wisdom, too, can be found in the words of the great physician of Western Islam, Moses Maimonides. A Jew, born in Cordova, he flourished during the twelfth century, just as the sun was setting on Arabic influence in Europe. He taught that the patient must be treated as a whole and humbly recognized his therapeutic limitations. 'This disease has many aetiological aspects . . . it cannot be managed without a full knowledge of the patient's constitution as a whole . . . furthermore I have no magic cure to report.'

Often an illness is seen in a new light when the physician is himself the sufferer. Jean Baptiste van Helmont born in Brussels in 1577 is perhaps remembered most for discovering carbon dioxide. This gas, produced by fermentation and combustion, he named 'gas Sylvestre' (woodland gas). Van Helmont was a practising doctor and himself had asthma. He described vividly the sporadic nature of the attacks of breathing difficulty. Likening them to the fits of epilepsy, he called asthma 'the falling sickness of the lungs'.

Two English physicians in the second half of the seventeenth century wrote at length and sensibly about asthma: Thomas Willis and Sir

What is asthma?

John Floyer. Willis viewed asthma as alarming: 'There is scarce anything more sharp or terrible than the fits thereof.' Though his ideas on lung function were firmly Galenic his observations have a curiously modern flavour. 'Whatsoever therefore makes the blood to boyl or raises it into an effervescence, as violent motion of the body or mind, excess of intern cold or heat, the drinking of wine, venery, yea sometimes mere heat of the bed, doth cause asthmatical assaults to such as are predisposed.'

Floyer suffered under the 'tyranny' of asthma for thirty years. 'The asthma is a laborious respiration with lifting up the shoulders and wheezing . . . , 'tis observed that the asthmatic cannot cough, sneeze nor speak easily, because a sufficient quantity of air cannot be drawn into the lungs to produce those actions.'

Both Floyer and Willis, drew a distinction between 'convulsive' or 'periodic' asthma and 'pneumonick' asthma. The 'pipes of lungs' had been described by this time and there was an awareness that these air passages, the bronchi, were implicated in asthma. Of periodic asthma Floyer wrote: 'I have assigned the immediate cause of the Asthma to the straightness, compression or constriction of the Bronchi', and Willis wrote that asthma was due 'to cramps of the moving fibres of the bronchi'. Pneumonic asthma they recognized as a more continuous illness associated with obstruction of the bronchi by 'thick humours'.

It is interesting to reflect that when John Floyer and Thomas Willis were writing about asthma they had no idea of the true function of the lungs. They believed, like their predecessors, that air was drawn into the lungs to cool the blood. Not until the second half of the eighteenth century did Antionne Lavoisier conclusively demonstrate that a gas, named by him oxygen, was removed from the air by breathing and that this gas was essential to life. So slow was the advance of medical science in these times that if experiments carried out by Willis' contemporaries, Boyle and Mayow, had been rightly interpreted, similar conclusions could have been reached more than a century earlier.

We have the advantage over our eighteenth-century predecessors in possessing a very detailed knowledge of anatomy and physiology. It will thus be helpful at this stage to look a little more closely at the way in which the lungs are constructed and the way in which they work. One lung is situated on each side of the chest. Each has a sponge-like structure. The spaces in the sponge—there are about 300 million of these—connect to the outside through a series of branching pipes through which the air passes: these are called the bronchi. Blood is supplied to the lungs from the right side of the heart and returned to the left side of the heart.

What is asthma?

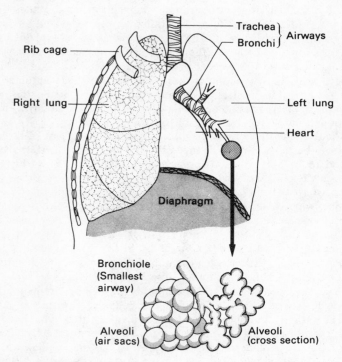

Fig. 1. The lungs, showing how they are situated inside the chest, with some details of the airways and air sacs.

The lungs fill most of the space within the chest. A slight vacuum holds them out against the inner wall of the rib cage. Air is drawn into the lungs and expelled from them by the action of muscles in the chest wall. The muscles between the ribs widen the rib cage when breathing in and narrow it during breathing out. Beneath the lungs lies the most important muscle for breathing, the diaphragm. When it contracts it pulls downwards, sucking air into the lungs. When it relaxes, the lungs recoil back to their resting position.

The muscles of breathing are unique amongst the body's musculature. They can be moved at command but also operate automatically. We can fill our lungs full of sea air. We can hold our breath to keep out smoke. We can shout or sing. The use of the muscles of breathing in

What is asthma?

these ways is akin to the use of arm or leg muscles for writing or walking. But whereas arm and leg muscles remain stationary unless we will them to move, the muscles of breathing do not. They have an automatic or involuntary rhythm of their own. Whether we are dozing in a chair or running for a bus, the muscles of breathing keep up their regular movement. In this respect they are behaving like the muscles of the heart. Heart muscle action is, however, almost wholly automatic and we have very little, if any, voluntary control over it. So the unique nature of the muscles of breathing lies in their dual control, for the most part automatic, but available for voluntary use.

The task of the breathing apparatus is the movement of air in and out of the lungs. From the incoming air, oxygen is transferred to the blood to be pumped around the body by the heart. From the blood, carbon dioxide—the waste gas produced from the use of the oxygen—is transferred to the air in the lungs and so breathed out. By ingenious devices which detect the level of both the oxygen and carbon dioxide in the blood, the brain regulates the degree and rate of movement of the chest, so that just the right amount of oxygen is supplied for the moment-to-moment needs of the body. In sleep, breathing is slow and shallow because little oxygen is required. In exercise, large quantities of oxygen are needed: so breathing is rapid and deep.

The movement of air into the lungs is through the bronchi. Entry is through a single tube, the trachea or windpipe. The trachea is some 10-12 cm long and about 2 cm wide. It divides into two main branches — the major bronchi — which supply the right and left lungs. Division then continues more or less regularly 10 to 25 times ending with thin flexible tubes of about half a millimeter bore. Off these the 300 million air sacs, or alveoli, bud, so that their external appearance is very much like bunches of grapes. The internal surface of these numerous air sacs is vast, sufficient if spread out to cover an area about the size of a tennis court.

The blood vessels supplying the lungs also divide up from a single supply vessel but in nothing like so regular a fashion. They branch into a myriad of tiny thin-walled capillaries coursing over the surfaces of the air sacs. Through the thin walls of the alveoli, the blood in the capillaries picks up oxygen and gives off carbon dioxide, to be returned, replenished to the heart.

It is with the bronchi that the trouble lies in asthma. The air sacs are spaced and if air gets to them they behave normally. *If* the air gets to them; for in asthma it may fail to do so. In asthma there is narrowing or actual blockage of the bronchi. This abnormality is the basis of the cardinal symptom of asthma, wheezing.

What is asthma?

Bronchial narrowing may be caused in several ways: by mucus, poured into the bronchii by swelling of the internal layers of the bronchii or by contraction of the muscle lying in the walls of the bronchi which leads to constriction of the air passages. These three mechanisms for narrowing the airways need to be looked at in greater detail.

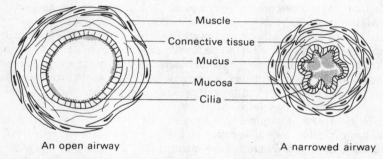

An open airway   A narrowed airway

Fig. 2. The detailed structure of the airways.

Like most surfaces of the body, the bronchi have several layers. The lining layer, known as the bronchial mucosa, is very thin. Its surface cells point inwards. They are lined by extremely fine hairs. These hairs, or cilia, beat in rapid motion up towards the mouth carrying with them a thin layer of mucus. Particles of dust inhaled into the lungs are caught up in the mucus layer and so are carried by the wafting action of the cilia away from the deeper parts of the lung. The mucus itself is produced by other cells in the lining layer, some of which are collected together in clusters, the mucous glands. It seems likely that one of the ways in which narrowing of the airways occurs in asthma is by an excess production of mucus: or perhaps by an inefficient action of the cilia in ridding the lungs of mucus.

The lining cells sit on a layer of rather nondescript tissue which acts as a packaging material. It is a tissue that lies beneath many body surfaces and which allows a certain amount of movement. Pick up a piece of skin over the back of the hand, for example, and you will find you can move it backwards and forwards over the underlying muscles and bones. A similar flexibility exists beneath the surface layers of the bronchi. Because this is a loose layer of tissue, it can readily become swollen. Thinking again of the skin; after a bee sting, a swelling appears. This consists mostly of fluid derived from the blood. Swelling of the tissues beneath the lining layer of the bronchi occurs during asthma.

23

What is asthma?

It is another cause of narrowing of the airways. In the severest asthma attacks, this swelling can be so great that it pushes the surface lining off. This, in combination with thick sticky mucus, can produce a plug which actually blocks the airway, rather than just narrowing it. Throughout most of the airways there is beneath these linings a muscle layer. The strands of muscle wind spirally around the airway so that when they contract they squeeze the airway and so narrow it. Contraction of bronchial muscle occurs in asthma. It can be the sole factor causing airway narrowing. In this case, the change in calibre is usually short-lived, perhaps lasting only a minute or so. It often occurs together with swelling and mucus production to cause a more persistent airways narrowing lasting several hours. Contraction is not quite the appropriate word for this prolonged shortening of muscle, and the term bronchospasm is used.

A great deal of emphasis has been laid on bronchospasm as a cause of bronchial narrowing. The trap in using this term is to suppose that all the narrowing is due to muscle spasm and so to neglect consideration of other components such as the swelling and mucus just described. Nonetheless there are important reasons for this emphasis on muscle contraction. Much more is known of the mechanisms controlling muscle activity than of those responsible for mucus secretion or mucosal swelling. It can be studied experimentally. But most of all, there is a practical reason why this emphasis has occurred. It is a therapeutic one. As we shall see later, many of the most effective remedies used in asthma have been designed to relax bronchial muscle.

So we are now in a position to formulate an answer to the question posed at the heading of this chapter 'what is asthma?'. Asthma is a condition characterized by episodes of breathing difficulty due to widespread narrowing of the airways of the lungs. This narrowing can be due to mucus in the airway, to swelling of the lining of the airway, or to spasm of the muscle in the walls of the airways, or to a combination of all three.

It may be questioned whether asthma should be regarded as a disease in its own right, or whether it is merely a symptom of some other disorder. This hinges very much on defining the word disease. Taken in a colloquial sense, it implies a state of disturbance: disturbance from what is generally regarded as normal; indeed disturbance in a disadvantageous direction. The description of a disease begins with symptoms, the reporting of what brings dis-ease. The physician, basing his observations on many patients, will try to delineate the disorders of body structure and function that accompany this state of disease. Finally,

What is asthma?

working with his scientific laboratory colleagues, the physician will, it is hoped, be able to identify a cause for the bodily disturbance and so for the disease.

This hierarchy of analysis can be applied to any disease. A simple example is the complaint of a sore throat. On a symptomatic level the disease is simply that: a sore throat. In anatomical terms 'throat' would be translated into Greek to describe the structure involved: the pharynx. To describe the functional abnormality, namely inflammation, the ending, 'itis' is added, so the combination: 'pharyngitis'. If laboratory tests demonstrate an invading micro-organism in the throat, a bacterium such as the streptococcus, a full categorization from symptomatic state to causation can be packed into the disease definition, 'streptococcal pharyngitis'.

How far this procedure can be applied to asthma will become apparent throughout this book. The symptomatic description is satisfactory and can be condensed into 'episodic wheezy breathlessness'. the structural site of the disease is the lungs, and the functional change is to do with a narrowing of the air passages. The explanations of the means whereby this narrowing is brought about are various and it will emerge later that even in a given individual, it may not be possible to pinpoint a single cause for his asthma. Causation appears to be multiple—and this opens up questions about a possible underlying disturbance that renders the lungs liable to respond in an asthmatic way to many and various insults.

It is worthwhile at this stage disposing of one or two other words which are either used in connection with asthma, or get confused with it. The word has remained attached to the breathing difficulties experienced by some patients with heart diseases until this day. 'Cardiac asthma' is a quite separate problem from 'true asthma' or 'bronchial asthma' so that most physicians have dropped the term. When used as a word on its own, asthma means bronchial asthma, and this condition, which has nothing to do with heart disease, is the subject of this book.

Bronchitis is a term that frequently crops up in connection with wheezy breathlessness. The 'itis' has been noted to mean inflammation. So bronchitis is inflammation of the bronchi, the air passages in the lungs. In acute bronchitis the inflammation is caused by an infection, most often a virus infection. Acute bronchitis may occur in subjects with asthma. When it does so, an attack of asthma may be triggered. Sometimes asthma occurs only when there is an infection present and this situation may be labelled wheezy bronchitis or asthmatic bronchitis.

What is asthma?

Chronic bronchitis is rather different. The agent causing the inflammation in chronic bronchitis is not an infection; it is atmospheric pollution. For the most part the culprit is that very personal atmospheric pollution caused by cigarette smoking, though industrial pollution can play its part. These forms of pollution work slowly and over a long time; they are chronic. The damage they cause to the air passages results first in coughing. With coughing, phelgm is produced and chronic bronchitis means simply that: chronic cough with the production of phlegm. Air passages damaged in this way are prone to infection. So, added to the chronic inflammation, there may be episodes of acute bronchitis.

Patients with chronic bronchitis may eventually become short of breath. This is first noticeable on hurrying or climbing stairs. It is an extension of the effects of inflammation on the air passages. The way in which this operates is in some respects similar to that discussed for asthma and the disorder is somewhat akin to Willis's 'pneumonick asthma'. But the breathing difficulties of the chronic bronchitic tend to be slowly progressive and not obviously spasmodic. So they do not generally earn the label asthma.

One reason for the inexorably progressive course of the breathing difficulties in this type of patient is the concurrent development of emphysema. Emphysema is a destructive process whereby the lungs gradually lose their resilience. Cigarette smoking is again the chief cause. Patients with emphysema become very short of breath. But this is not asthma.

2

How is asthma recognized?

THE sensations engendered by a disease are all too familiar to those who suffer from them. To describe those sensations to another is not so easy. Even with pain, one of the most commonly experienced symptoms, it is never certain that the sharpness of a pain will mean quite the same to one person as it does to the next. With breathing difficulties, words seem more than usually inadequate. Perhaps this is because of close links, both biblically and in the popular mind, between breath and life. To take away the breath is to threaten life itself. Such fundamental sensations are not easily described.

Most of us, most of the time have the good fortune to be unaware of our breathing. It is true that exercise can be pushed to the lengths of producing shortness of breath even in the fittest individual. Breathing during exercise is both deeper and more rapid than when resting. There is a certain rawness in the chest—which is due to a drying up of the surface of the air passages and can be relieved by breathing moist air—but the sensation is not unpleasant. Until the point of exhaustion is reached, there is a feeling of satisfaction, that the breathing is meeting the demands placed on it by the exercising body.

None of this is the case with the asthmatic. The presence of bronchial narrowing slows the movement of air into and out of the lungs. More effort is required to achieve an adequate flow of air and this increased effort intrudes itself into consciousness. The greater effort produces a sense of difficulty in breathing, which is at the very least unpleasant and can be frightening.

In asthma there is more difficulty in breathing out than in breathing in. This is partly because during breathing in, as the lungs expand, there is a pull on the airways tending to widen them. During breathing out the reverse is true. So the airways are relatively more narrow during breathing out. In addition, whilst a normal breath out is a passive affair requiring little effort, in the presence of narrowed airways, greater effort is required, more muscles are brought into use, and so more difficulty is sensed.

The breathing difficulties of the asthmatic are thus not merely an accentuation of sensations that the healthy amongst us experience during exercise. They are qualitatively different, and demand the use of different descriptive words. Three such words in common use by asthmatics are tightness, congestion, and wheeze. They all refer in some way to that fundamental change in asthma: narrowing of the airways.

The chest tightness experienced by the asthmatic is a direct detection that the airways have narrowed, and that greater effort is required to move air through them. It is an unpleasant sensation that provokes anxiety.

Like many words used to describe symptoms, 'congestion' means one thing to the sufferer another to the doctor. To the medical profession it has a well-defined meaning relating to an unnatural retention of fluid in tissues, and an entrenched tradition connecting this with heart disease. The patient has no such precise ideas in mind when he describes his chest as congested. To him it implies a filling up with phlegm that needs clearing. As such it can be a sympton of asthma. It is also a symptom of several other lung (and heart) conditions.

Wheeze is an onomatopaeic word, perhaps more obviously so in its Old Norse origin 'hvaesa' which meant hiss. It is the audible evidence of air being forced through narrow airways. Regularly heard through the stethoscope, a wheeze can become obvious to both the asthmatic subject and his attendant in a sharp attack of asthma.

Patients may also try to put into words the sensation of distention of the lungs which is consequent on the difficulty in getting air out through narrowed airways. A New Zealand physician who had been a lifelong asthmatic remembered describing this sensation as a child in these words: 'It's just as if your chest had been blown up with a bike pump and then put into a iron clamp.'

It is not so much the symptoms themselves as the circumstances under which they occur that makes asthma so readily recognizable. Tightness in the chest, a congested cough, and even wheezing can all occur in other diseases. In asthma it is characteristic that they occur in paroxysms. These may be either brief episodes of chest tightness lasting a matter of minutes, or more prolonged episodes of wheezing lasting up to an hour or so, which merge into a full-blown attack of asthma.

The asthmatic recognizes that his lungs are sensitive to the weather. Despite warm clothes, the cold winters air 'catches' his chest. There is an immediate tightness, a momentary shortness of breath, but it quickly passes off. The change from a cold outside environment to the warmth of the house might produce a similar brief episode of tightness. There is sensitivity also to the fumes of petrol, gas fires, wood smoke, cigarettes, and so forth. If exposure is sudden and brief, the tightness is transitory.

How is Asthma Recognized?

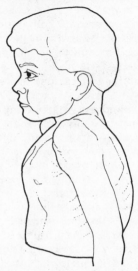

Fig. 3. A child with asthma illustrating the distended chest and raised shoulders.

If the fumes build up slowly, so may the tightness and be all the more bothersome in the end for so doing. The asthmatic is wary too of violent movement of the chest, as in coughing and laughter. Both can set up a paroxysm of wheezing.

These episodes are all examples of the extreme sensitivity of the asthmatic's airways to irritant stimuli. These are not asthmatic attacks— but they are brief episodes lasting perhaps a few minutes of tightness, wheezing, coughing, shortness of breath, that plague the asthmatic's life. It is uncommon for these types of irritation to set off a more prolonged episode of wheezing. This usually requires a stronger stimulus. Perhaps one of the best documented is exercise. Aretaeus', second century description of asthma begins, 'If from running, gymnastic exercise or any other work, the breathing becomes difficult, it is called asthma.' Shortness of breath during exercise is a common complaint in many types of chest disease. There is however something rather different about the effect of exercise on the asthmatic, which almost certainly escaped the notice of Aretaeus. Though the asthmatic does become short of breath during exercise, much more importantly, he becomes even more short of breath after exercise has ended. Instead of being able to relax and 'get his breath back', he finds that a rapidly progressive

How is Asthma Recognized?

paroxysm of wheezing overtakes him. It reaches its peak within a few minutes and he may not recover for half an hour. Virtually no other type of chest disease is associated with breathlessness which gets worse immediately after exercise, so that this symptom is an extremely valuable guide to diagnosis.

The effects of irritants and of exercise illustrate two aspects of the variability in symptoms that is the hallmark of asthma. There are other patterns. One of the commonest is the waxing and waning in wheeziness which occurs during the course of the day. Many asthmatics will comment on a bothersome tightness in the chest and wheezing soon after awakening in the morning. With or even without the help of morning medicines, the tightness eases in an hour or so, and the rest of the day can be troublefree.

An accentuation of this characteristic is for asthma to make itself known during the night. Sir William Osler writes, 'Nocturnal attacks are common. After a few hours sleep, the patient is aroused with a distressing sense of want of breath and a feeling of great oppression in the chest.' There is very often a short irritating cough which fails to produce any phlegm. Breathing is an effort. Muscles around the neck and shoulders are brought into play. There is an obvious and audible wheeze. Sitting up brings some relief and often fitful sleep can follow until with the dawn the attack settles, and, exhausted, a few hours sleep can be snatched. Paroxysms of wheezing like this, repeated night after night, are often associated with a more general wheeziness during the day. This phenomenon of wheeziness in the small hours of the morning or on awakening has become known as the 'morning dip' and is a very important feature of asthma.

These fluctuations are superimposed on much broader patterns of change that vary considerably from subject to subject. These patterns depend to a great extent on certain specific circumstances which appear to trigger a more prolonged episode of wheezing. They may be seasonal, as with the asthma that accompanies summer hay fever. They may be intermittent as with infections. They may be either brief or more prolonged with emotional stresses. The details of the circumstances which trigger these attacks form the subject matter of later chapters. Whatever the cause there are certain features common to all attacks which are worthy of mention.

Before an attack there may be premonitory symptoms. Aretaeus again: 'The symptoms of its approach are heaviness of the chest, sluggishness to one's accustomed work.' Others describe mood changes, often irritability, which is difficult to rationalize, mixed with depression or apprehension. In a few there is forced gaiety of mood. Before wheezing becomes obvious, coughing is common, not only in attacks at night, but also at other times. It is irritating, rarely productive. Skin irritation with an insatiable urge to scratch is described by some. It especially affects the front of the upper chest. As there will be cause to discuss later, nasal symptoms are commonly associated with asthma. If these have taken the form of a blocked nose, there is a remarkable tendency for the nose to clear early in an asthmatic attack.

At the height of the attack, the dominant feature is the paroxysm of violent wheezing dyspnoea. The sufferer is pale, his facial expression anxious. Beads of sweat stand out on his brow. He feels cold: his skin is clammy. His pulse is rapid and with each breath in, the pulse fades, recovering its force as the breath in is achieved. The soft tissues around the neck and between the ribs are sucked in with the effort of breathing. He sits forward, elbows on knees, or arms resting on the edge of a chair or bed, gasping for breath. Speech is almost impossible save for short broken phrases. He is restless, frightened, and distressed.

One curious feature of the more severe attacks of asthma, rarely commented upon now but noted by earlier writers, is the passage of large quantities of pale urine. Sir John Floyer noted in in 1698. So did Dr Bree, another physician who himself suffered from asthma. The chemical analysis of urine not having been introduced in 1798, Bree remarks, 'I have tasted the water of an asthmatic more than once . . . I have always found it weak, saline and of no saccharine taste whatsoever.' (By the latter remark he was distinguishing this from the copious sugary urine passed by a diabetic).

Many attacks of asthma settle spontaneously: most · today, are aborted by medication, and fortunately few proceed to the extent described by Aretaeus, 'If these symptoms increase, they sometimes produce suffocation after the form of epilepsy.' The easing of an attack is noticed first by the patient himself. The sense of distension is the first to go. It becomes possible for him to breathe out more freely. The wheeze will remain for a while, or even increase its loudness as the air flows more easily. Secretions are released; there is both salivation and productive cough. The phlegm is clear of whitish, sometimes frothy, often sticky and tenacious. It may contain dense white pellets or strands, which occasionally have a branched appearance. They represent casts of mucus which have lodged in the smaller bronchi and have been released as the attack subsides.

After the attack the tension relaxes, the mood elevates. Drink is demanded, some have a great hunger, all want rest.

How is Asthma Recognized?

Whilst the attack is the hallmark of asthma and the bronchial irritability a common feature, there is in a few asthmatics a more general
shortness of breath on exertion. Harping back once more to the eloquent description by Aretaeus, 'During remission, although they may
walk erect, they bear traces of the affection . . . (there is a) difficulty
of breathing in running or on a steep road.' This is thus activity-limiting
shortness of breath, perhaps associated with wheezing, often not. A
patient will say, 'It is not my asthma, I'm just short of breath.' This
seems to imply that the anxiety-provoking tightness and distension of
the attack are lacking. Due to some permanent, but not rapidly variable
narrowing of the airways, it is that much more difficult to produce the
increased flow of air necessary for activity.

The process of recognizing any disease depends first on obtaining
an accurate story. The description just given is the basis on which
asthma will be recognized. In an individual much more detail will be
required of the circumstances which provoke an attack, in order to
identify causes: but more of this anon. Beyond the story, the physician
will want to obtain objective information that he can himself gather
which will not rely on the subjective sensations of his patient.

There is much in the description just given that is observable. He will
note the manner of breathing, the effort put into it, the muscles used,
the position adopted. He will note in mild or early stages of an attack,
the prolonged breathing out phase, which may slow the overall rate
of breathing. He will note in the more severe attack the increased rate
of breathing and the overinflation of the chest. He will check the pulse
for its rate and any variation in its force through the breathing cycle.
He will tap the chest to hear the drum-like resonance of lungs distended
with air. And he will listen with the stethoscope. Breathing in will be
sharp, breathing out prolonged. Whistling sounds will assail his ears.
Laennec called them râles—literally 'rattles'. Those heard in asthma
were moist râles, those in many other chest diseases dry râles. But the
sounds in asthma were not really a rattle, even one filled with water.
Laennec tried as an alternative 'rhonchi' from the Greek 'rhogchus' (to
snore) but even this had a rattling connotation that did not really describe the sounds. When the whistles were of high pitch 'sibili' was the
preferred word.

In recent years some have gone back to the Old Norse root and are
using wheezing to describe not only the generally audible sounds of
asthma, but also the sounds heard with the stethoscope. Rhonchi,
sibili, wheezes are heard in all asthmatics with narrowed airways. In
very mild asthma they may only be audible after exercise or on forced

How is Asthma Recognized?

breathing. In very severe asthma they may become very soft because so little air is flowing. Sounds of this sort are heard in other disorders affecting the chest. In deciding whether the sounds he hears are due to asthma the physician will look back over his story to make sure that it fits, and will supplement what he hears with the stethoscope with some objective tests of breathing that aim at measuring the calibre of the airways.

Measurement becomes necessary because the memory so easily plays tricks with the subjective recall of symptoms experienced previously, and because the degree of shortness of breath varies so widely in different subjects with similar degrees of airways narrowing. Some objectivity can be given to the recording of symptoms by using the 10-centimeter line technique. A line (Fig. 4) is provided which relates to a range of symptomatology—for example breathlessness—from 'worst ever' at one end of the line, to 'best ever' at the other. The patient is asked to mark on the line a point representing how he feels at the time, in relation to the two extremes.

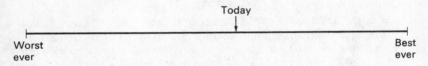

Fig. 4. The 10-cm line used for recording the severity of symptoms.

Such a technique allows numerical comparisons to be made of symptoms on different days. It does not however replace objective measurement of airways calibre. Indeed simultaneous assessment of symptoms using the 10-centimeter line and function, using tests about to be described, may show striking discrepancies—both in the direction of a more serious functional disturbance than the patient had imagined, and vice versa.

Direct measurement is, of course, impossible in a living subject. It is in any case doubtful if measurements of the diameter of the airways would be useful for there are so many of them. In health they vary in diameter from 2 cm to a fraction of a millimeter, and can be widened or narrowed as the whole lung is inflated or deflated. It is not a structural measurement that is required, but a functional one. The airways are used as passages for conducting air to and from the gas-exchanging surface of the alveoli. They function dynamically and should be tested dynamically. In normal airways, air should flow quickly and easily. If

How is Asthma Recognized?

the airways are narrowed, as in asthma, the potential for flow along them will be impaired.

The principle of the most widely used test of airways function is to assess the maximum capacity for the airways to conduct the flow of air. This is done by stressing the system. Air is forced through them by the bellows action of the chest wall. The lungs are slowly inflated to their maximum extent. The breath is held for a moment. The air is then forced out as fast and completely as possible. The test finishes when the lungs have been emptied.

The efficiency with which this forced breathing out manoeuvre is carried out can be assessed in various ways. One of the very simplest is to measure how long it takes to deliver this complete lung full of air. All the equipment that is needed is a watch and a good ear, perhaps aided by the stethoscope to listen over the front of the chest for the last traces of air flowing. The time taken is directly related to the degree of narrowing of the airways. A healthy adult will expel this air in about two seconds and will rarely take more than three. If the airways are narrowed, flow is slowed. The time taken is often prolonged to 5 or 6 seconds and it may be 12 seconds or more.

It might well be argued that the time taken to deliver a lung full of air will depend on the amount of air in the lungs. It does to a degree. This volume can, of course, be measured. The volume of air which can be expelled from the lungs from a point of full inflation to one of maximum deflation is known as the vital capacity (VC). The lungs are not completely empty of air at the end of such a breath. A limit is imposed, chiefly by the bony structure of the rib cage, which clearly cannot be compressed beyond a certain point.

The vital capacity can be measured by any one of various devices, known as spirometers. Most spirometers in current use consist of a plastic bellows housed between two hinged metal sheets. Air blown into the bellows will displace the sheet and this movement can be registered to give a measure of volume (see Plate I).

The size of the vital capacity varies considerably from person to person. It is obvious that a large person is likely to have a greater vital capacity than a small one. Height must therefore be taken into consideration. There is an aging effect. Irrespective of height, the lungs are largest in the teenage years. In adult life there is a steady decline in size with advancing years. Finally, men have larger lungs than women of the same height and age. So, in order to obtain some idea of the vital capacity to be expected in a given individual, consideration must be given to height, age, and sex. Using these, a predicted value can be arrived at.

How is Asthma Recognized?

Nonetheless normality still lies within quite a wide range around this predicted value, usually taken to be 20% either side. For a predicted vital capacity of 4.0 litres, values between 3.2 and 4.8 litres would be within normal limits.

Very often the vital capacity is normal in asthma. If sufficient time is taken, a full deep breath out will deliver a vital capacity within the normal range. In severe asthma the vital capacity does decrease. This is more noticeable when the vital capacity is delivered forcibly than when it is delivered slowly.

But neither measurements of time, nor measurements of volume, alone give sufficient information about the rate of delivery of air in the forced expiratory manoeuvre. All spirometers are geared so that volume can be charted against time. This tracing is known as a spirogram. The slow progress in delivering the air through the asthmatic's narrowed airways now becomes very obvious. The simplest and most useful measurement is to look at the volume delivered after one second. A normal subject will deliver 70 per cent or more of his total vital capacity in one second. Narrowed airways will slow this down. So the asthmatic will deliver less than 70 per cent of his vital capacity in one second. It may be 50 per cent: it can be as low as 20 per cent. The actual volume delivered in one second—the forced expiratory volume (FEV_1)—will depend therefore on the degree of narrowing of the airways. It will also depend, of course, on the size of the vital capacity which in its turn depends on the factors outlined above. This is why it is useful to quote the FEV_1 as a percentage of the VC. Thus from the spirogram delivered by the asthmatic, measurement is made of the one second volume, the FEV_1, and of the total volume delivered, the VC; and the percentage the one represents of the other is calculated: the FEV_1/VC per cent.

A careful look at a spirographic tracing whether from a healthy subject or from an asthmatic will reveal that the rate of change of volume is very rapid in the first few fractions of a second after the breath out has commenced. Thereafter, the curve flattens out as the rest of the vital capacity is delivered. Rate of change of volume is, of course, flow. And really it is the flow down narrowed airways that is of greatest interest. At the very beginning of the breath there is no flow. Flow then rises very rapidly to a peak value. Thereafter, it declines slowly over the ensuing seconds, until again, when all the air has been expelled, flow is once more zero. Devices exist for charting flow throughout the forced breath, but as with the volume trace it is possible to choose one point which gives a useful index of the pattern of change. The obvious choice with flow is the peak. Simple

How is Asthma Recognized?

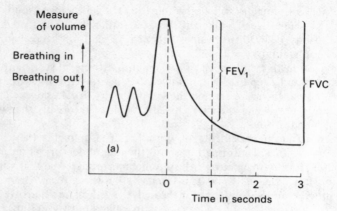

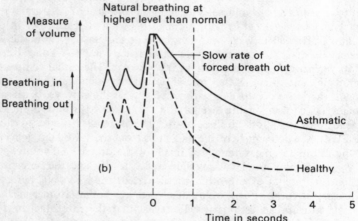

Fig. 5. Charts depicting volume of breath moved during natural breathing followed by the full breath in and forced breath out used to assess airways narrowing. (a) Tracing typical of healthy subject; (b) Tracing in asthmatic subject compared with healthy subject.

measuring devices have been devised which record flow and which lock when the peak value has been reached (see Plate I). They are known as Peak Flow meters and the measurement is called the Peak Expiratory Flow (PEF). These meters are the commonest devices used to measure lung function in relation to asthma in general practice and also in hospital. Normal values lie between 400 and 600 litres/min and, like the

How is Asthma Recognized?

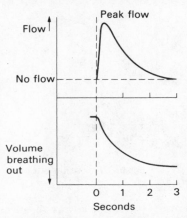

Fig. 6. Simultaneous tracings of flow (above) and volume (below) during a forced expiration.

measurement of vital capacity, depend on height, age, and sex. In asthma values between 200 and 400 are common and in severe attacks peak flow may drop to 100 litres per minute or even lower. The peak flow machine has proved an ideal tool for measuring the fluctuations in airways' narrowing from hour to hour that are such an important feature of asthma (Fig. 7).

Objection can be levelled against tests which depend, as those described so far, on the forced expiratory manoeuvre. The very young, who have not yet learned how to use their breathing muscles, will not be able to perform properly. The elderly may find that their powers of control have waned. The very anxious, the mentally disturbed, and the unconscious will not be able to carry out these tests. Cooperation is essential, for to get accurate and meaningful results the breath must be a full one from maximum inspiration to the bottom of expiration and it must be forced out with the greatest possible effort. Together with all this there is a scientific objection, that properties of the lungs other than the calibre of the airways influence the result of the test. Perhaps the most readily comprehensible of these would be a consideration of the lungs inherent elasticity. This aids recoil of the lungs back to their resting position. If the lungs are less elastic than usual some decrease in the rate of recoil might be anticipated. But despite all these objections, there is no doubt whatsoever that spirometric and peak flow measurements based on the forced expiratory manoeuvre have

How is Asthma Recognized?

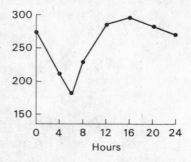

Fig. 7 Chart showing typical asthmatic variation in peak expiratory flow during a twenty-four hour period.

contributed enormously to the objective assessment of the asthmatic patient. Above all they are simple to perform, commendably reproducible, and employ cheap and often portable equipment.

Other means for evaluating lung function in asthma exist. They are all less easy to perform and usually employ sophisticated and expensive equipment. They do however throw light on the functional disturbances that occur in asthma and so are invaluable for research. It is useful for example to be able to measure the resistance offered by the airways to the flow of air through them during quiet breathing. This may be done using a plethysmograph, a large airtight box with a glass side in which the subject sits (see Plate II). The plethysmograph can also be used to measure the total size of the lungs including the air left in the lungs after a deep breath out. This reveals that in asthmatics the lungs are blown up. The difficulty in getting air out means that air remains inside, so the lungs become distended. In mild asthma a modest increase in lung volume may compensate for a slight narrowing of the airways. This is because, as the lungs distend, so do the bronchial tubes. In more severe asthma, overexpansion of the lungs is an important cause of distress.

Techniques such as these just described are not routinely employed. They give a clearer picture of the overall disturbance of the functioning of the lungs in asthma, but they are not essential for day-to-day management. For this the peak expiratory flow or the one-second forced expiratory volume are entirely adequate.

The recognition of asthma thus depends on a carefully taken story describing the features of the attacks of wheezing and shortness of breath. It depends too on observation. And it is confirmed by measurement.

38

How is Asthma Recognized?

Both subjective and objective information taken together build up the picture which we recognize as asthma. The circumstances under which asthma occurs provide clues to the cause of asthma. In the next few chapters some of the mechanisms provoking attacks of asthma will be looked at. First, the fact that asthmatic airways are irritable. Next the question of allergy and a description of a variety of other trigger factors including infection, the emotions, and occupation.

3

Irritable airways

CENTRAL to the subject matter of the next few chapters is the question 'what is the cause of asthma?'. It is a question that admits no single answer. Already we have seen that asthma is due to a narrowing of the bronchial airways. This narrowing is caused by mucus, by swelling of the lining of the airways, by bronchial muscle spasm. But what causes the mucus production, the swelling, the spasm?

Some answers can be provided by looking at the circumstances, generally regarded as provoking or triggering an attack of asthma—allergy, infection, and emotional stress. These will all be covered separately in subsequent chapters. Before looking at these specific examples, it is important to recognize that in asthma there appears to be an underlying general irritability of the airways—not only to the major triggers just mentioned but also to rather less specific insults such as the breathing of cold air or fumes, laughter, and exercise.

It has already been hinted that the brief episodes of wheezing that follow such stimuli are likely to be due almost exclusively to spasm of bronchial muscle with little or no contribution from mucus or swelling. So what are the forces controlling the contraction and relaxation of bronchial muscle?

It will be recalled that bronchial muscle is involuntary muscle. It cannot, like the muscles of arms or legs, be contracted at will. The nerves which send their fibrils out to serve involuntary muscle make up what is known as the autonomic nervous system. This part of the nervous system regulates the activity of muscle in the heart, bowel, and bladder, as well as bronchial muscle. It also regulates the secretion of glands in the bronchi, the skin, and the bowel, the calibre of blood vessels, the size of the pupils, and the functioning of many other internal organs.

The autonomic nervous system can be broadly divided into two parts, the sympathetic and the parasympathetic. The sympathetic nerves prepare the organism for what has been described as 'fight or flight'. The pulse quickens; the blood pressure rises. Blood is diverted from the skin and digestive organs to muscles and brain. The hair stands on end, muscles quiver, pupils widen, and the bronchi dilate. The parasympathetic nervous system on the other hand concerns itself with more leisurely digestive and restorative functions. The pulse is slowed and blood is transferred to the digestive organs. Muscles relax, pupils narrow, and the bronchi contract.

The conveying of information along a nerve and the bringing into activity of muscle are both achieved using a form of electrical energy. There is a small but definite gap between the nerve and the muscle. When it comes to the point of bridging this gap a chemical messenger, known as a neurotransmitter, takes over. Different chemicals subserve this function in different parts of the nervous system. For the sympathetic nervous system the transmitter is noradrenaline. For the parasympathetic nervous system it is acetylcholine. When we come to consider the treatment of asthma, attention will need to be directed towards chemicals that cause relaxation of bronchial muscle. For the moment the reverse is true. Our present concern is with what causes bronchial muscle to go into a state of contraction. Clearly one way in which this could occur would be if the parasympathetic nervous system was brought into action. There is now a considerable amount of evidence to suggest that this is just what happens during brief episodes of wheezing and chest tightness, such as occur when the asthmatic inhales fumes, or moves from a warm room out into the cold air.

Parasympathetic nerve pathways in the lungs are activated by what is known as a reflex. Reflexes are one of the ways in which the human body responds to external stimuli. They are inbuilt, automatic responses and are not consciously instigated. Information received by a sensitive nerve ending is transmitted through central parts of the nervous system and converted into activity that is in some way appropriate to the particular stimulus. There is sometimes a conscious awareness associated with reflex activity. The dropping of a hot plate is a reflex action, but the signal soon gets through that our fingers are burnt. Other reflexes, such as those controlling balance, posture, and movement, operate almost exclusively without our awareness of them.

The most readily understood example of a reflex involving the lung is coughing. A crumb 'goes down the wrong way'. It lands on the surface of the large airways. Here it excites nerve endings. These send messages to the brain which call forth an explosive contraction of the muscles of the chest so that air, and with it the offending crumb, is

Irritable airways

forcibly expelled from the lungs. This reflex is thus, like dropping the hot plate, a protective mechanism. The nerve fibres leading from surface nerve endings in the airways up to the brain, and those passing back down again to the bronchial muscle, are bound together in a bundle known as the vagus nerve. This nerve is one of the most important parts of the parasympathetic nervous system.

When surface nerve endings further down the airways are excited, the response is not a cough, not a contraction of the muscles of breathing around the chest, but a contraction of the muscles in the walls of the airways. So the airways narrow. At first sight this bronchial reflex response again seems to be protective. It attempts to protect the depths of the lung from unwanted particles of dust and irritating fumes, making it more difficult for them to penetrate through narrowed airways. But it also makes it more difficult to breathe them out again. Thinking more carefully it becomes obvious that narrowing the airways is not by any means the most efficient way of coping with unwanted inhaled irritants. Furthermore why does it happen so much more readily to the asthmatic than to the person with healthy airways?

Bronchial irritability—the tendency of the airways to narrow in response to inhaled irritants—can be studied objectively. Measurements are made of the degree of bronchial narrowing with the subject resting quietly. A breath or two of some irritant is then given. Further measure ments are made repeatedly over subsequent minutes. If sufficient irritant has been given and the airways are sufficiently sensitive, then the measurements will show an increase in the degree of airways' narrowing. Its extent and duration can be charted. One subject can be compared with another by recording the dose of irritant required to cause a predetermined change in the calibre of the airways.

Using a test procedure such as this, known asthmatic subjects can be compared with subjects who have no asthma. In every instance, and no matter what sort of irritation is used, the airways of asthmatics are more sensitive than normal. In some instances the difference is very striking, of the order of several thousand-fold.

What sort of irritants have been tested in this way? The list is long. It includes changes in the physical characteristics of the air breathed, (for example its temperature), irritating dusts and fumes, certain specific chemicals, and many substances thought to be responsible for allergy. Chemicals and allergy will receive their mention in due course; uncomplicated irritation will be considered first.

One means of providing a physical stimulus to the bronchi is the taking into the lungs of a deep full breath. In the asthmatics such a

Irritable airways

manoeuvre causes a brief but dramatic increase in airways' narrowing. It can be detected within 15 seconds of the deep breath and is usually gone within a minute. This mechanical reflex bronchial narrowing is parallelled in the everyday life of the asthmatic by the wheezing that may follow laughter, or be initiated by coughing. A breath of cold air, a cloud of dust, or a whiff of smoke can all be tested similarly.

When an asthmatic is well, and free of wheezing, it is often difficult to demonstrate bronchial irritability in response to physical irritants. However, when the asthmatic becomes wheezy, for whatever reason, then the irritability returns. Such an observation suggests that the difference between subjects with asthma and those without it may just be a question of degree. It suggests that the detection of irritability requires the presence of some initial narrowing. The relationship need not be, and probably is not, a linear one. A waterfall provides a useful analogy. Measurements can be made of the height of a river above sea level. One mile upstream from a waterfall, the difference in height on moving downstream to just above the waterfall is miniscule. On the other hand, from that point onwards, for a very small distance moved downstream, there will be a dramatic difference in the height of the water above sea level (see Fig. 8).

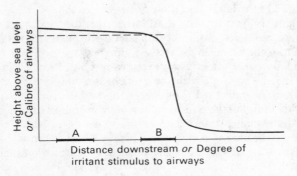

Fig. 8. The waterfall, illustrating the effect of a journey downstream (or an added irritant stimulus to the airways): A, well upstream (healthy airways) and B, on the brink of the waterfall (asthmatic airways).

So it may be with the airways. The calibre of the airways corresponds to the height of the water. The distance moved downstream represents the challenge provided by the irritant. The subject without asthma sits well upstream away from the waterfall. The irritant has very

43

Irritable airways

little detectable effect. The asthmatic, on the other hand, teeters on the brink of the waterfall. A similar dose of irritant will send him tumbling over into an asthmatic attack.

These considerations of the geometry of the airways go a long way towards explaining bronchial irritability in the asthmatic. Whether they explain it entirely is by no means certain. One major alternative explanation centres on the notion that in the asthmatic, there is a fundamental disturbance of autonomic nervous system control over bronchial muscle. It seems plausible that in the airways there is normally a healthy balance between sympathetic and parasympathetic influence such that the calibre of the airways is appropriate for an easy flow of air in and out of the lungs. A hyper-irritable vagal reflex component would cause an imbalance in the autonomic forces in favour of the parasympathetic system, at least in the bronchi, if not elsewhere in the body. Indeed towards the end of the last century asthma was called a 'vagotonic' disease.

A refinement of this general idea, introduced more recently, suggests an imbalance within the internal forces that regulate the sympathetic nervous system. The importance of these apparently obscure arguments lies in trying to discover whether any imbalance that can be demonstrated is an inherited characteristic or whether it arises as a result of the disorder. In the latter case it might be preventable.

Returning to the irritability itself rather than theories about it, many studies have used, not physical stimuli acting through reflexes, but chemicals. Those chosen are known to be intimately involved in the chemistry of muscle contraction. They excite very powerful reactions in the airways, and the way in which the bronchi respond to these chemicals has shed considerable light on the nature of bronchial irritability.

The chemical deserving note at this point in the narrative is acetylcholine, the chemical transmitter in the vagus nerve which is responsible for the bronchial irritability reflex. When a solution of acetylcholine is made into a vapour and inhaled, it causes bronchial muscle to contract. Most tests for assessing this have employed a compound closely related to acetylcholine, namely methacoline. Results from inhalation tests with methacholine demonstrate a dramatically increased bronchial irritability in the asthmatic. It requires a great deal of methacholine to persuade normal airways to narrow, whereas asthmatics' airways tighten very readily. It seems likely that when the methacholine is inhaled, it penetrates through the bronchial wall and so comes into direct contact with bronchial muscles. Not surprisingly, the muscles tighten, and so the airways narrow.

44

Irritable airways

A close study of the results of bronchial irritability tests, however, reveals a situation that is not quite as straightforward as might have been hoped. As a symptom, irritability of the airways has been seen to be a hallmark of asthma. But it turns out that there are subjects with disorders of the airways other than asthma who also show undue irritability to methacholine. Most common amongst these are smokers. Prolonged cigarette smoking renders the bronchi irritable. Yet this is not asthma. Bronchial irritability can also be demonstrated in otherwise healthy persons who develop a chance acute bronchitis due to a virus infection, as will be discussed more fully later. So whilst bronchial irritability is a striking feature of asthma, it is not exclusive to it.

The increased narrowing of the airways which follows the inhalation of irritants is short lived and self-limiting. Very occasionally it persists for longer. The contrast between the pattern of wheezing which has been discussed so far and more prolonged episodes of wheezing is more clearly illustrated by exercise-induced asthma. In the last chapter it was noted that breathlessness which comes on, or gets worse, after exertion has ended, occurs in no other condition. It is understandable therefore that a considerable amount of effort has been expended in trying to understand the mechanism for this type of asthmatic wheezing.

During the course of exercise it is rather difficult to make accurate measurements of airways' calibre, but what information is available suggests that in most people, including asthmatics, the airways widen during exercise. It is what happens after exercise that provides the crucial difference. In the normal subject the airways quickly settle back to their previous state, never narrowing by more than 10 per cent. In the asthmatic this is not so. If serial measurements are made every minute, there is observed a sharp decline in airways' calibre. The airways reach their narrowest between about three and five minutes after the end of exercise, remain at that level for a while, and then gradually widen again. The pre-exercise calibre is usually restored within about an hour but some degree of increased narrowing can persist for two or three hours. The extent of the change can be considerable. A decrease in airways' calibre by 20 per cent would not be unusual, and the response may be a reduction to over half the initial level.

Exercise can be taken in many forms, and not all appear to be equally potent stimuli for exercise-induced asthma. Sir John Floyer remarked two centuries ago that for the asthmatic: 'the most agreeable exercise is riding'. Running is certainly the worst. Six to eight minutes free running is recommended when testing for exercise-induced asthma, but many asthmatics will become wheezy with a shorter duration than

Irritable airways

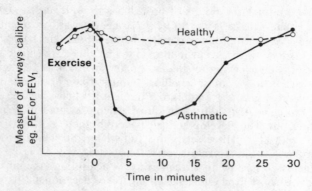

Fig. 9. Airways' responses of an asthmatic and a healthy subject to exercise.

this. Bicycling will also induce asthma though somewhat less consistently, perhaps because only the legs are used. Kayak paddling, which only uses the arms, is only a mild stimulus. Swimming seems to be the most innocuous of all and so can be recommended to asthmatics. Although both arms and legs are used in swimming, the weight of the body is supported freely by the water. Thus it may be that it is a question of the total amount of energy used that is important in inducing asthma after exercise.

The differences between these forms of exercise are important both to the doctor studying asthma, and, of course, to the patient. In everyday life, the asthmatic will find that the severity of exercise-induced asthma is less with shorter periods of exercise and with light as opposed to heavy exercise. Quite hard exercise, for example playing football, can however be tolerated by the asthmatic, provided it is in brief bursts with some respite in between. Almost all asthmatic children have exercise induced asthma: it is less common in adults.

How does exercise induce wheezing? This remains a mystery. Medicines which relax the bronchial muscles, if given before exercise, will prevent the development of wheezing after exercise. So the muscles must be involved. They are probably stimulated to contract by the local release of chemical substances. That some sort of chemical mediator is involved is supported by the fact that a second exercise test carried out within two hours of one test, will produce a much smaller response. This implies that the first test has depleted the stores of some mediator, and that it takes time for these to be replenished. A small

46

rise in the level of histamine in the blood has been demonstrated after exercise-induced asthma. So perhaps this is responsible.

Histamine is another of the chemical substances that have a special place in asthma. Like acetylcholine, it seems to be involved in the mediation of spontaneous asthmatic episodes; and asthmatic airways are unduly irritable to histamine as they are to acetylcholine. Inhalation challenge tests can be carried out in asthmatics using histamine in the same way that was described for methacholine. Again, asthmatics are much more sensitive than normal subjects, but wheezy smokers may be unusually sensitive as well. The release of histamine is especially important in allergic asthma, which will be considered in the next chapter. How exercise causes histamine release is not known.

Before leaving the question of the chemical causes of asthma, there is one other group of substances that deserves mention. These are known as the prostaglandins. They have attracted a good deal of attention recently because of the possible light they might throw on the intimate chemical changes that cause asthma, and also because they appeared to offer an explanation for an unusual trigger mechanism for asthmatic wheezing—taking aspirin. A very small proportion of asthmatics, perhaps 2 per cent to 4 per cent, notice that aspirin causes them to wheeze. This is not an allergy to aspirin. None of the tests for allergy, such as will be described in the next chapter, are positive. Furthermore it is not a specific reaction. Subjects sensitive to aspirin are often also sensitive to other substances that are chemically quite unrelated to aspirin. These include other pain-killing medicines and also tartrazine and benzoic acid, agents used as food additives, in flavouring and colouring.

All these substances do seem to have one significant property in common. They all suppress a chemical production line that results in the formation of prostaglandins. Prostaglandins are found all over the body. They are of many different types and have many different actions, some beneficial, others probably not. One of the unpleasant features of prostaglandins is that they seem responsible for certain sorts of pain. The reasons for the effectiveness of certain analgesics, such as aspirin, may therefore lie in their ability to suppress prostaglandin production. Prostaglandins released in the lung affect the bronchial muscle. One prostaglandin causes powerful contraction: another is a rather weak relaxant of these muscles. So when produced together the effect of the powerful one is dominant. The muscle contracts and the airways narrow.

Asthmatics have been tested for their response to inhaled prosta-

Irritable airways

glandins in the same way that challenge tests have been devised for histamine or methacholine. All asthmatics are exceptionally sensitive to the powerful prostaglandin which very easily triggers an asthmatic episode. When aspirin-sensitive asthmatics are compared with other asthmatics, then the prostaglandin produces less, not more, bronchial muscle contraction. So, having begun with the idea that aspirin-induced asthma might be triggered by a chemical reaction involving prostaglandins we arrive at a rather anomalous position. First, aspirin and allied drugs turn out to suppress rather than encourage the formation of prostaglandins. Secondly, the sensitivity of the airways to prostaglandin seems to be less in aspirin-sensitive than in other asthmatics. Despite this, the research undertaken has revealed an alternative mechanism for producing asthma—prostaglandin release—that is neither mediated by nervous pathways, nor is allergic in origin.

The conclusion to be drawn from this rather difficult discussion, which has necessitated excursion into nervous system control and muscle chemistry, is that the airways of the asthmatic possess a rather remarkable irritability. Not only does the inhalation of special chemicals excite a brisk narrowing of the asthmatic's airways, but so does the accidental breathing of dust particles, fumes, and smoke. Even such commonplace disturbances of the even ebb and flow of air in the lungs, as laughter or exercise, can be followed in the asthmatic by embarrassing wheezing and tightness in the chest. This irritability represents a disturbance of the behaviour of the airways that almost certainly lies at the root of much of the asthmatic's trouble.

4

Pollens, mites, and moulds

IT is widely recognized that asthma may be due to allergy. So what is allergy? Allergy is an enhanced sensitivity, an unusual reactivity. The word was coined at the beginning of this century by Von Pirquet. He used it to describe 'an altered capacity of the body to react'. He was thinking particularly of the body's reaction to the injection of material from other living creatures.

Perhaps the first observation of altered reactivity in this sense was that of Edward Jenner. He introduced the idea of smallpox vaccination in 1798. This was based on the observation that the inoculation of a woman who had previously had cowpox, with material from a patient with smallpox, produced, not a potentially fatal disease, but simply a mild rash. She exhibited an altered reactivity to the pox virus. It was specific: it did not apply to other viruses such as that of influenza. The altered reactivity depended on previous exposure to the virus. It was thus acquired. The altered reactivity was, in this example, beneficial. Not only was it beneficial to the one woman described by Jenner but his observation led to the subsequent virtual eradication of smallpox by vaccination, and so has been to the benefit of all mankind.

Whilst the altered reactivity is always both specific and acquired, it is not always beneficial. Von Pirquet specifically excluded any reference to benefit from his definition of allergy, because he had in mind experiments conducted at about that time which showed that repeated injections of foreign material, instead of producing less, sometimes produced greater ill effect. This was shown to be true for poison from the diphtheria organism, and for more innocuous seeming materials such as serum from horse's blood. Over the years there has been a tendency to reserve the word allergy for these adverse reactions and to use the word immunity for beneficial reactions. But the words are interchangeable and in recent years it is customary in scientific circles to talk of the study of all types of altered reactivity as immunology.

In asthma the altered capacity to react lies in the lungs. It is not natural for the airways to narrow when foreign material is inhaled. By their very nature the lungs are constantly exposed to foreign particles and fumes present in the air we breathe. The reaction produced in the asthmatic is unpleasant and causes difficulty in breathing. It is difficult

49

Pollens, mites, and moulds

to regard it as beneficial. Like the response to repeated injections of foreign material, it is an acquired, altered reactivity. It is also a specific, altered reactivity, though a given asthmatic may be abnormally reactive to more than one foreign substance.

In the context of allergy, these foreign substances are known as allergens. Allergens are nearly always proteins. If they are not, they seem to attach themselves to a protein in the blood before they can set up altered reactivity.

Allergy in asthma depends on the production by the body of new proteins which have a specific capacity for recognizing their appropriate allergen. These proteins are termed antibodies. The antibody produced against pollen grains is specific. It will not react with horse serum, diphtheria toxin, or any other foreign material. There are other forms of allergy in which antibodies are not involved, but these seem unlikely to be involved in asthma as far as is known at present, and can therefore be disregarded.

There are two types of allergy implicated in producing asthma. They differ in the pattern of illness to which the reaction gives rise and in the nature and location of the specific antibodies that are formed. The commoner of these produces a reaction within a matter of minutes and is known as 'immediate' allergy. This will be described first. The other type, 'late' allergy, gives a reaction only after several hours.

Immediate allergy is commonly known as atopy. Subjects who suffer from it are described as atopic. It is the misfortune of a relatively small proportion of the population—about 10 per cent—to have severe atopy, though many others have lesser degrees of atopic sensitivity. Coca, who introduced the term atopy in 1923, used it to describe patients with a variety of conditions which tended to occur together and which all seemed to be due to an altered reactivity. Asthma was chief amongst these conditions. Others were infantile eczema—an irritative inflammation of the skin especially in the creases of the elbows and behind the knees: allergic rhinitis—sneezing, running of the nose, and watering of the eyes suggesting a 'cold' but due to allergy: and urticaria 'hives' or 'nettle-rash'—raised red lumps that appear in the skin and itch violently. Coca also added several other conditions to his list such as migraine and high blood pressure which today would no longer be accepted as atopic.

The altered reactivity which is the hallmark of atopic allergy in these patients is reflected in a special sensitivity of the skin. However, whilst subjects who are atopic in terms of skin sensitivity are quite likely to have asthma or allied atopic conditions, they do not all have such disorders. Equally, whilst subjects with asthma may well be atopic in

Pollens, mites, and moulds

terms of skin sensitivity, by no means all of them are. Because of this. skin sensitivity rather than any particular condition, such as asthma or eczema, is now considered the basis for the designation atopic.

Atopic skin sensitivity is demonstrable to certain allergens found commonly in the environment—fragments of animal hair, pollen grains, components of household dust, moulds, and so forth. Extracts or solutions can be prepared from these materials. A drop of the fluid is placed on the skin of an atopic person. A prick into the surface layers of the skin beneath the drop will allow a minute amount of fluid into the skin. Providing there has been prior exposure to that allergen a sensitivity reaction will follow within 15 minutes. The skin becomes itchy, then red. Finally a small weal, usually about half a centimeter across will form. This positive skin prick test signifies the presence of atopy (See Plate III).

In many instances a positive prick test in a subject with an allergic disorder means that the allergy is directly due to that particular allergen. Whilst this is not always so, it does represent the most straightforward example of allergic asthma. A young girl develops an interest in horses. After a few weeks with her horse she notices a ticklish cough and a tight sensation in the chest. Next she is a little out of breath on running to catch the horse. Then after a vigorous grooming and brushing session she becomes obviously wheezy and distressed. When her skin is tested with horse hair extract there is a positive reaction. The child has asthma. She is atopic. Her asthma is directly triggered by her allergy to horses.

What is happening in her lungs? The allergen from the horse is inhaled by the child. It enters the body through the thin surface layer of the airways. There it is encountered by cells that recognize it as foreign. Antibodies are formed. These are antibodies to the horse hair. They are of a type specifically produced by the atopic subject, and called IgE (immunoglobulin, class E). Very little of this antibody is released into the circulation, though modern techniques can detect an excess of IgE in the blood of atopic subjects. Most of the antibody clings to the surface of rather specialized cells known as mast cells. These cells are amongst those that migrate around the body. When they settle down they tend to choose the lining tissues of the bronchi and the skin.

The child inhales horse hair particles again. They meet, in the lungs, mast cells coated by specific IgE antibody. Antibody and allergen combine together. This union is disruptive for the mast cell. Its cell wall breaks down and from the interior of the cell, granules are released into the surrounding tissues. These granules contain a complex array of chemical substances, which have a wide variety of effects. Enough can

51

Pollens, mites, and moulds

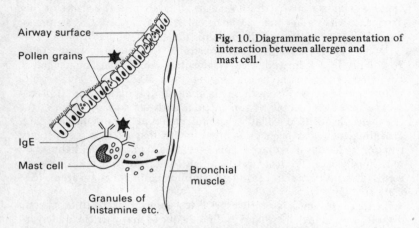

Airway surface

Pollen grains

IgE

Mast cell

Granules of histamine etc.

Bronchial muscle

Fig. 10. Diagrammatic representation of interaction between allergen and mast cell.

be understood about the development of asthma under these circumstances by considering just one: histamine. This substance has at least two actions relevant to the production of asthma. It causes fluid to leak out of small blood vessels into the loose connective tissues lying beneath the surface of the bronchi. The tissue swells and so the bronchi are narrowed. But also the histamine stimulates the bronchial smooth muscle causing it to contract. Once again this narrows the bronchi. Other substances released from mast cells probably have similar actions. A combination of effects from several chemical mediators prolongs the bronchial narrowing. With this type of allergy, exposure to allergen will produce wheezing that reaches its peak in about 10 minutes, and if there is no further contact with the horse hair will wane within an hour, and will not be obviously detectable after 4 hours (see Fig. 11).

Asthma in an atopic child sensitive to horses represents one of the simplest examples of allergic asthma. Allergy is a common feature in asthma and the situation is not always so simple. Indeed the allergies most frequently associated with asthma—to pollens, to mites, and to moulds—each illustrates special features about allergic asthma that repay further study.

Writing over 100 years ago a middle-aged man recalls a childhood experience, 'I was at the play-work of hay-making with my young companions, surrounded by newly mown grass, when I was suddenly seized with profuse lachrymation, swelling of the eye-lids, well-nigh blinding me, and ceaseless sneezing'. His description is of the allergy to grass pollen popularly known as hayfever.

Pollens, mites, and moulds

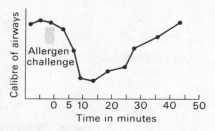

Fig. 11. Time course of response of tests for airways' narrowing following challenge with an allergen causing an immediate reaction.

Nasal hayfever is common, affecting perhaps one in ten of the population. Much less frequently, the hayfever is accompanied by asthma. This is often first heralded by coughing and chest tightness at night during the height of the hayfever season. Then there will be wheezing, day or night, or both. Often a curious reciprocal relationship develops between the chest and the nose. Whilst sneezing and running of the nose are prominent symptoms, the asthma is mild or non-existent. But if the nose becomes blocked, then wheezing builds up.

Grass pollen asthma most commonly first makes itself manifest in the first year or two of the hayfever. Both hayfever and purely seasonal grass pollen asthma have a characteristic age of onset. It is unusual for this sort of asthma to start in infancy. It generally begins to appear late in childhood and there is a broad peak of age of onset around puberty which then slowly falls off throughout the teenage period. This contrasts with the distribution of age of onset of asthma in general which has a marked peak in the first few years of life.

With four fifths of the land in England devoted to agriculture, grass pollens from Sweet Vernal, Meadow Foxtail, Timothy grass and a host of others are the usual causes of summer hayfever symptoms. The grasses of the rough pastures of the Scottish highlands and Welsh mountains produce less pollen and on the coast, sea breezes drive the pollens inland. By comparison with his country cousin the town dweller is to a certain extent protected against pollen exposure by the forest of stone and concrete that surrounds him.

The grass pollen season covers late spring and early summer. Smaller quantities of pollen are shed before and after this season, extending the period of suffering for unusually sensitive subjects into early spring or late summer. Symptoms parallel the presence of pollens in the atmosphere. They are greater on a dry, sunny and windy day and less when

53

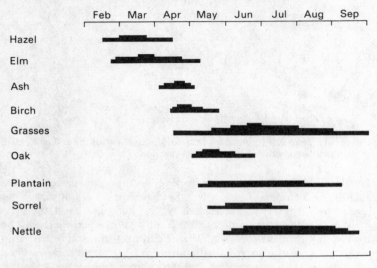

Pollens, mites, and moulds

Fig. 12. The seasonal distribution of some common pollens in Southern Britain (based on data from Cardiff collected by Drs H. H. Hyde and K. F. Adams, *Acta Allergoligica*, 1960).

rain dampens the spread of the pollen. Most common grasses shed their pollens in the morning, but on a hot day the maximum fall extends into late afternoon.

Tree and flower pollens are for the most part not important causes of summer seasonal nasal symptoms or asthma. Yet some individuals are sensitive. Trees flower early, sometimes before their leaves have unfurled. Sneezing and wheezing in early spring may be due to birch pollen: others implicated are elm, hazel, alder, maple, and so forth. Most decorative flowers are not wind pollinated. The scented flowers with their small number of sticky rough pollen grains are insect pollinated. So flower allergy is not common. Not so with weeds. In North America the commonest summer allergy is to ragweed. Symptoms are commonest in early autumn and have earned the name autumnal catarrh. In Great Britain weed allergy to plantain and sorrel may be admixed with grass pollen allergy. Nettle has a long pollen season with two peaks. One coincides with the grass pollen season and so is obscured. The other is later, so that allergy to nettle may account for some late seasonal allergies recorded in these months.

Pollen grains in the atmosphere can be collected, counted, and

54

Pollens, mites, and moulds

identified. Rather different pictures will be given on the same day by collecting devices set up in different localities. It is perhaps unfortunate that the top of a hospital roof in London has been chosen to record the pollen count which is broadcast and published each summer day for the information of the British public. Conditions vary so much from place to place that the London figure can be more confusing than helpful.

With all these summer allergies whether to tree, grass, or weed pollen it seems that only a small proportion of those affected by nasal symptoms will develop asthma: and none seems to have asthma alone without the nose being affected. Just why some subjects become asthmatic and others do not, is not known. Despite this, there are interesting similarities as well as differences between those who develop asthma and those who just have hayfever. The most striking similarities lie in the responses recorded to tests for allergy. Skin tests are not more strongly positive in those who develop asthma, neither is their response to bronchial provocation with pollen extracts.

This needs spelling out quite clearly. First, it is difficult if not impossible to create an artificial situation in the laboratory whereupon the inhalation of a dust of free pollen grains will induce wheezing. Secondly whilst it is possible to induce wheezing with pollen extracts, the amount of extract necessary to create even a small degree of asthma can be greater than the total amount of pollen antigen inhaled naturally in the whole season. Subjects with hayfever alone will respond to this extract by wheezing even though they do not get asthma in the pollen season, at a dose only slightly greater than that required to produce wheezing in those who naturally develop asthma as well as hayfever. So, although symptoms only develop during the pollen season, challenge tests with pollen or pollen extracts do not seem to be a good way of reproducing what is happening naturally.

Despite this, there is one important and probably fundamental difference between subjects with hayfever only, and those with hayfever and asthma. This is the response to inhaled chemicals. In describing the chemical events involved in the production of the airways narrowing that is characteristic of asthma, two important chemicals were mentioned, histamine and methacholine. It will be recalled that asthmatic subjects were found to be unduly sensitive to these chemicals. With metacholine provocation, subjects with hayfever alone are just a little more sensitive than normal subjects. But those with asthma as well as hayfever are dramatically more sensitive, of the order of a hundred-fold or more. Furthermore methacholine and histamine

Pollens, mites, and moulds

challenges produce much more striking effects during the pollen season than out of the season. So the presence of pollen grains in the atmosphere somehow creates the state of increased airways irritability that seems such an essential feature of asthma. But why it does so in some subjects and not in others remains a mystery.

Asthma occurring with hayfever makes itself obvious by its strictly seasonal occurrance. When asthma is related to an antigen that is ubiquitous and present all the year round, the relation of the asthmatic symptoms to the presence of antigen is much less obvious. Such is the case with household dust. Dust is of course, a complex mixture. It contains fragments of animal and man-made fibres, skin scales, particles of minerals, decorating material, wood, foods, materials such as moulds and pollen blown in from outside, and living creatures, especially insects. The major arthropods are all too familiar to the housewife; she abhors the spider and curses the woodworm. But in the microcosm of household dust are a myriad of tiny mites that escape notice with the naked eye. Of these the commonest is a member of the Pyrglyphid species, *Dermatophagoides pteronyssinus* (See Plate IV). This creature is that commonly referred to as the house dust mite—though closely related mites can also be embraced within this title. It is probably the most important component of household dust as far as asthmatics are concerned.

D. pteronyssinus is about 0.3 mm long, ellipsoid in shape with eight legs. The female is a little longer than the male and lives longer too. Its life-cycle from eggs through to the end of its adult life is up to six months. The mites like a warm damp environment. Around 25°C proves ideal for breeding. Few mites survive long at temperatures less than 5°C. If relative humidity is less than 50 per cent they are quickly dessicated and if above 80 per cent they are suppressed by mould overgrowth. The peak season for live mites to be found is late summer and early autumn, and the trough early spring. And for food they relish human skin scales. They are not parasitic and only feed on shed scales. Since each of us sheds about 1 gram of skin debris in 24 hours, there is plenty of nourishment around.

Mites are found wherever man rests for long enough for his skin scales to collect; in the corners of living rooms, on carpets, in cushions and most of all in bedding. *D. pteronyssinus* mites make up over 90 per cent of the mites in bedding. There may be 3000 mites in one hundred grams of mattress dust. They congregate especially in seams and under tapes and buttons. Their life there is almost entirely unmolested by predators. Few insecticides can penetrate a mattress sufficiently well to kill off a significant number, though some success has been recorded with Paragerm. New mattresses can be kept free of mites by covering them with plastic. Hospital mattresses remain free because of the frequent cleaning, and changing of bedding and occupants.

Doubts were expressed about the precise significance of challenge tests in subjects with summer pollen asthma. Solutions made up from pollen grains gave reactions in sensitive subjects. Inhalation of natural pollen grain dust did not. Household dust has rarely been used as such in an attempt to provoke asthma. Many extracts of dust and of house dust mites have been used. As with the pollen extracts these create in the sensitive subject an immediate reaction. There is coughing and chest tightness within 10 minutes. Airways' narrowing is most marked between ten and twenty minutes and passes off spontaneously in one to two hours. This then is the characteristic immediate allergic response following the same time course as that of the skin prick test.

Challenge studies of this sort have an invaluable place in furthering understanding of allergic asthma, but they can only mimic natural exposure to allergen in certain circumstances. The child and her horse are a good example because exposure to the allergen is brief, the wheezing so induced compelling the victim to escape as quickly as possible. Pollen allergy sometimes behaves this way—as when the asthmatic wanders into a meadow in early summer: but more often it is a general tendency to wheeze throughout the pollen season. House dust allergy in its natural form is farthest removed from the simple challenge test. Whilst dust mites may be concentrated in bedding, they are everywhere. They can be found in the atmosphere at all seasons. The lungs are presented, not with a brief challenge to be followed by an immediate reaction, but by a continuous challenge which gives rise to a persisting state of variable wheeziness. It is important to grasp this point, for it is highly relevant to an understanding of the different patterns of behaviour seen in naturally-occuring asthma.

Whilst it has not been considered safe to deliberately prolong exposure to dust allergens, it has been feasible to follow some subjects for a longer period than the first hour after house dust challenge. During the second and third hours after the challenge, the chest tightness passed off. But then after about four hours in some subjects, it returned. This second phase of asthma could last several hours and be altogether a more troublesome reaction than the immediate reaction so far described.

These observations were by no means the first to demonstrate a late asthmatic reaction. In fact, they represent an extension into the

Pollens, mites, and moulds

field of dust allergy of studies on allergy to moulds that date back to 1873. This was the year of the publication of Blackley's book on Catarrhus Aestivus (summer catarrh or hayfever). In it he describes the unpleasant outcome of an accidental bronchial challenge resulting from the tipping over of a sample of moulds. He writes, 'After the sneezing had continued a couple of hours, the breathing became very difficult from constriction of the trachea or bronchial tubes . . . . In the course of five to six hours I began to have aching and a sense of weariness over the whole body . . . . I felt as if passing through an unusually severe attack of influenza.'

Moulds are members of the fungus family. Unlike mushrooms and toadstools they grow on a relatively small scale producing colonies of growth, often just a few millimetres across, on decaying vegetation and damp walls. Most of the moulds do not have common names, nor are they easy for the layman to identify. Penicillium, producing its furry greenish mould on Camembert and Roquefort cheese, is easily recognized. But it is rightly remembered much more as the source of the first antibiotic, penicillin, than as a cause of asthma. Dry rot is also easy enough to recognize. It has a characteristic musty smell and causes a red dust on furniture when its spores are shed in the autumn. These spores, when released into the atmosphere and inhaled, can cause asthma.

Most of the moulds that are important for the asthmatic are less conspicuous. Cladosporium and Alternaria moulds give brownish or grey patches on dead wood or indoor walls. From late summer into autumn very high counts of spores from these moulds can be found in the atmosphere in southern Britain, and many asthmatics who have late summer symptoms seem to be sensitive to them. Spore counts are highest in the warm parts of the day and, like the grass pollen counts, fall in wet weather.

Other moulds are encouraged by the damp and do not have a seasonal pattern. In damp climates these moulds can be found in almost all places at all times of year. Of these the Aspergillus species has been especially singled out for study because of its importance in asthma. Aspergillus moulds form grey or black patches on damp walls and very high counts have been found in compost heaps and rotting leaves. In each patch is a branching network of tiny fibres. Sticking out from this are stalks capped by a 'Mop' containing the spores (see Plate IV). The name of the mould indeed comes from the Latin, aspergillum, which was a mop used to sprinkle holy water in Roman Temples!

Aspergillus seems to take an especial pleasure in causing inconvenience

Pollens, mites, and moulds

to human lungs. For many asthmatics it is one of the potential groups of common environmental antigens, like pollens and the house dust mite, that can initiate the immediate type of asthmatic wheezing. But it is also the commonest cause of late reactions, which can result in more severe asthma.

During late reactions as Blackley described, there is a general upset as well as wheezing, a feeling of malaise, feverishness, and aches and pains of a flu-like nature. In fact aspergillus may make itself first known by what appears to be influenza occuring in an established asthmatic. Cough is a prominent feature and very obvious plugs of mucus, perhaps brownish in colour can be brought up. Aspergillus, unlike other airborne spores, will grow at body temperature and often the mucus plug will contain the mould. Settling in the lungs these plugs of mucus can block off an airway. No air can then penetrate into that part of the lung: so it temporarily collapses and evidence of this can be seen on the chest radiograph. When the mucus plug is coughed up, the lung reexpands and the chest radiograph clears.

These late reactions are also a form of allergy. IgE immunoglobulin is produced as in immediate allergy but also, due to the growth of the mould in mucus plugs, a different class of antibody is manufactured, IgG immunoglobulin. IgG antibodies do not attach themselves to mast cells but circulate freely in the blood. Antibody and antigen combine to form an immune-complex. This complex then appears to activate a series of chemical reactions which lead to the release of toxic substances, among them histamine, resulting in swelling of the tissues in and around the bronchi, and bronchial muscle contraction, so that the airways narrow. However, now, in addition, other substances attract scavenger cells which crowd in on the site of the allergic reaction. Cells and tissues break down and die and the products of cell death can cause local damage. Much of this damage can subsequently be repaired but there seems to be a greater chance of permanent tissue damage with IgG-mediated reactions and so the development of chronic asthma.

Whilst immediate allergy occurs within ten to fifteen minutes of inhaling allergen, the onset of late asthmatic reactions is delayed for two to six hours. This delay makes the relationship between exposure to the allergen and the development of wheezing, all the more difficult to detect. An immediate reaction passes off in a few hours, but a late reaction lasts much longer—at least twenty-four hours and sometimes thirty-six to forty-eight hours (see Fig. 13). Immediate reactions require very small quantities of allergen but late reactions appear only after exposure to large quantities of allergen over a considerable time.

Pollens, mites, and moulds

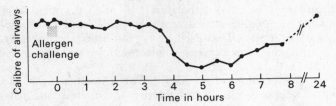

Fig. 13. Time course of response of tests for airways' narrowing following challenge with an allergen causing a late reaction.

Immediate allergy is common in a small subsection of the population—the atopic subjects. Late allergy can occur in anyone given sufficient quantity of allergen, and time of exposure. It seems to be especially important in occupational asthmas as we shall see later.

Allergy emerges then as an important trigger for asthmatic episodes. Immediate allergy may give short-lived attacks in response to allergens such as animal hairs and danders: there may be seasonal wheeziness with pollen asthma: or there may be more persistent asthma in those allergic to house dust. All these allergens are found commonly in the environment, but asthma as a response to them is only observed in specifically atopic subjects. More prolonged attacks due to late allergy can occur in both atopic and non-atopic subjects, and are due to a build-up of common allergens such as moulds or to rather more unusual allergens encountered in special circumstances. Some two-thirds of asthmatics seem to have at least some of their attacks triggered by allergy and a great deal is now understood about allergic mechanisms. The other major trigger factors, infection and emotional stress, are both as important as allergy, though less is known of the way in which they cause wheezing. They now have to be considered.

5

Wheezy bronchitis

PARENTS frequently report that their children's asthma is triggered by infection. 'When he gets a cold it goes straight to his chest, and he starts wheezing.' Many adults too, especially the more elderly, attribute attacks of asthma to infection.

What is infection? What is the evidence that it can cause asthma?

Infection has to do with the invasion of the privacy of our bodies by microorganisms, minute primitive living things. Best known of these are the bacteria and viruses. Each bacterium consists of a single cell protected by a tough outer coat. Viruses are just small fragments of a cell and can only survive and reproduce by residing in another living cell. Microorganisms are found everywhere. Their food requirements are minimal but their survival is critically dependent on environmental conditions. They reproduce by simple division.

Microorganisms in the atmosphere can settle on the skin but unless they enter the body through a cut or abrasion, they are innocuous. They may be breathed in: a few penetrate into the lungs, whilst most settle in the throat or nose. The surface layers of the nose and throat are quite delicate and frequently abraded. Organisms may reside here without causing trouble, but quite often they gain a foothold, enjoy the conditions, and start to breed. The result is a cold in the nose or a sore throat. The surface lining of the airways is more fragile than that of the throat, but its defences against infection are powerful so that the microorganisms which penetrate this far, rarely survive for long. If invading microorganisms do manage to defeat defence mechanisms in the airways, the result is bronchitis or pneumonia. Bronchitis is a street battle. If the battle is carried into the houses, into the depths of the lung, this is pneumonia.

Sore throats, colds in the nose, bronchitis, and pneumonia are all examples of infection. A growth of microorganisms is the essential feature. Inflammation with swelling, redness, pain, and an outpouring of mucus is the result. Defence mechanisms are mobilized and a battle ensues between the microorganisms and scavenger cells sent in to fight the infection. The debris from the fray colours the mucus yellow or green. Poisons absorbed from the infected site bring fever, malaise, aching, and listlessness to the rest of the body.

61

Wheezy bronchitis

The milder infections of the organs of breathing are due to viruses. The common cold is an example. It is often due to a rhinovirus (literally nose virus), but many other viruses may cause cold symptoms. Unfortunately there is seldom a clearcut pattern of illness which can readily be attributed to a specific virus. Everyone is familiar with the influenza virus. It can cause anything from a mild headache, through sore throats and bronchitis, to a prostrating illness with pneumonia. Very often a viral illness is complicated by bacterial infection. The disruption caused by the virus creates a fertile field in which an implanted bacterium can happily grow. The prolonged sinus catarrh after a head cold and the persistent coughing up of yellow phlegm after influenza, are both examples of this. Less frequently, bacterial infection alone can cause either a sore throat, bronchitis, or pneumonia.

The majority of episodes of nose and throat infections are nothing more than a bothersome inconvenience. Of those that 'go onto the chest' to cause bronchitis, a majority are, again, minor illnesses. They are characterized by soreness of the chest, cough, and yellow phlegm, but nothing more. It is in a small but important minority that there will also be wheezing.

This concurrence of wheezing with bronchitis is most frequently observed in asthmatics. As many as three out of every four asthmatics regard infection as a definite trigger mechanism for their wheezing. Before unreservedly accepting this view it must be pointed out that it is notoriously difficult to decide on symptoms alone whether an asthmatic episode has been triggered by infection or by allergy. A cold produces sneezing with running and blockage of the nose. So does the nasal allergy that may well accompany allergic asthma. Bronchitis produces coughing with the production of phlegm: so can allergic asthma. Allergic symptoms tend to occur recurrently each time the allergen is encountered. Infections are also sporadic afflictions. An infective bronchitis may give fever and aching limbs and the nasal discharge can become yellow. These last features are not seen with allergy: yet they are hardly firm criteria on which to differentiate infection from allergy.

More objective information is not easy to acquire but is vital in distinguishing these two. The offending microorganism can be sought in the case of infection. Unfortunately this is frequently a virus and techniques for catching viruses and persuading them to grow in the laboratory are not too reliable. Antibodies may be sought in the blood. After a recent infection the level of specific antibody to the virus rises temporarily.

Wheezy bronchitis

Despite these difficulties, it is now possible to pinpoint whether infection or allergy is responsible for a given episode of wheezing. When this is done it emerges unequivocally that infection can, and frequently does, trigger an episode of wheezing in an asthmatic. These attacks of wheezy bronchitis are especially common in asthmatic children and seem to be caused more often by rhinovirus infection than by other viruses.

Many children with wheezy bronchitis seldom wheeze at other times. The relationship between recurrent wheezy bronchitis and asthma is a confusing one and one that has been subjected to close scrutiny. Primary-school children in Melbourne, Australia were examined at seven, ten, and fourteen years. Those with recurrent wheezing attacks and often persistent shortness of breath—the obvious athmatics—were divided off from those who had suffered just a few attacks of wheezy bronchitis, and those who had never wheezed. The asthmatics frequently gave a story of hayfever and eczema; skin tests for atopic allergy were almost universally positive. Those who had never wheezed rarely showed these features. But interestingly, those who had just had a few attacks of wheezy bronchitis fell in an intermediate position. They were more likely to show features of allergy than the non-wheezers, though never so frequently as the definite asthmatics.

Earlier, (page 46) it was noted that exercise tests have revealed bronchial irritability to be an almost universal feature of childhod asthma. Positive tests persist for many years after the asthma has cleared. It can also be shown that airways irritability, as judged by exercise testing, can be detected in some children who have previously just had wheezy bronchitis. Furthermore, there is an increased chance that the parents and brothers and sisters of these children will have both irritable airways and positive prick tests for atopic allergy. All this suggests that the tendency to airways irritabiltity might be inherited. Alone, it can predispose to wheezing with bronchitis. With other characteristics, again possibly inherited, it can lead to fully developed asthma.

Thus, wheezy bronchitis in children seems to be a very mild form of a condition that in more susceptible children would be called asthma. Quite how many wheezy episodes are needed to change the label from recurrent wheezy bronchitis to one of asthma is arbitrary. It will differ from physician to physician. Wheezy bronchitis in adults is rather more difficult to sort out in its relationship to asthma, and this will be reviewed later in Chapter 7. There is, however, no doubt that at all ages infection can and does trigger an episode of wheezing in the established asthmatic.

Wheezy bronchitis

In addition to this there is now evidence that bronchial infection can itself create conditions which encourage wheezing, conditions that did not exist before the infection had occurred, and indeed might not exist after the infection has finished. It can be shown that previously healthy subjects develop minor degrees of airways narrowing during a simple cold in the head. More significantly they show increased airways irritability. Whether tested with irritants, with specific chemicals such as methacholine or with exercise, there often appears during a virus bronchitis and for several weeks afterwards, an undue irritability of the airways.

No large-scale survey has been carried out on a healthy population suffering from virus infections to evaluate the extent of this increased irritability. It is almost certainly absent or mild in some, and symptomatically significant in only a few. What is of special relevance to the present discussion is the suggestion that one attack renders the sufferer more likely to further episodes of wheezy bronchitis.

This possibility receives most support from studies in very small children. From about three to six months of age, babies seem unduly susceptible to infection with a virus known as respiratory syncitial virus. These children develop coughing, wheezing, and distress that is in many ways similar to a severe attack of asthma. If carefully followed up over subsequent years, it seems that about half of these children will have further wheezy attacks, and these may be sufficiently recurrent to earn the label asthma.

Are attacks of wheezy bronchitis the same as other wheezy episodes, for example those set off by allergy? It is not easy to be sure about this. Certainly there are few asthmatics whose attacks are exclusively triggered by infection, or exclusively by allergy. So both occur in the same person. However, some patients seem to be able to distinguish bronchitis with wheezing from asthma. It is tempting to dismiss this by saying that they are latching onto clues—such as yellow phlegm in bronchitis—given them by the doctor. But at least one piece of objective information suggests that they may be right. This relates to the reversal of the wheezing by treatment. In the chapter on irritable airways, the potential for narrowing the airways—and so causing wheeze—through a reflex, was discussed. Lung reflexes can be blocked by the use of the drug, atropine. In allergic asthma atropine is rather ineffective. In wheezy bronchitis it can be very beneficial. This suggests that vagal reflexes might be more important in wheezy bronchitis than they are in allergic asthma. So whilst both wheezy bronchitis and allergic wheezing can occur in the same asthmatic person, they do not necessarily operate through the same mechanism.

Wheezy bronchitis

It is almost certainly too simplistic to suppose that when infection sets off wheezing it does so solely by vagal reflex irritability. Other possibilities have been explored. One of the more intriguing is that there is an allergic response to the infecting microorganism.

Part of the body's defence against microbial infection consists in creating antibodies. The stimulus for this antibody production comes from protein material in the bacterium or virus just as it does with pollen grains or house dust. Some viruses stimulate a very powerful antibody response. When this happens a subsequent attempt by the virus to invade that host is met with such resounding force that a second infection can rarely take place. This happens with measles, polio, and smallpox viruses. Other viruses are able to attack time after time. Some like the influenza virus achieve this by cunningly changing the colour of their spots from year to year. Yet other viruses, like the rhinovirus, seem to exist in so many distinct forms that immunity against one confers no protection against another.

The production of antibodies to invading microorganisms is largely thought of as a protective mechanism. But could it be damaging? Could an immune reaction between bacterial antigen and the antibody manufactured against it, be harmful? Could this harmful reaction take the form of asthma? There are no definite answers to these questions. The few facts available do not add up to a complete story. Indeed they suggest a field wide open for further investigations.

First, skinprick tests like those described for allergy have been carried out using extracts of bacteria. Employing just those bacteria which are naturally sitting around in the mouth and which might cause infection if the ground was primed by a virus infection, positive reactions are recorded in asthmatics more often than in the healthy. The reaction does not develop immediately, as for atopic allergy, nor yet after four to six hours as for late allergy. It is delayed twenty-four hours or more. This delay implies the operation of other types of allergic mechanism. No serious study of these mechanisms in the asthma which accompanies wheezy bronchitis has been carried out.

Secondly, certain bacterial infections given to experimental animals can modify their immunological responses. Whether this can occur in man is wholly unknown. Finally, in terms of the treatment of wheezy bronchitis in the asthmatic, antibiotics, which help to immobilize the bacteria, may not be effective if given alone: often therapy directed against allergic responses must be added. Vaccines have been prepared against the organisms which give positive skin tests. The use of these in the treatment of asthma was once greatly in vogue. They proved worthless and are rarely used today.

So the second major trigger for attacks of asthma, infection, almost certainly operates in a different way from allergy. Yet it too is capable of setting up a state of heightened irritabilty in the airways. Whilst this especially happens in asthmatics, it can also occur in hitherto healthy individuals. This raises the intriguing possibility that infection can actually initiate asthma in someone who previously did not suffer from it.

6

Emotion and personality

CRYING and laughter signify a close association between the emotions and breathing. Excitement and horror can cause us to catch our breath. Can the emotions cause wheezing? There is a long tradition that says they can. Hippocrates warned the asthmatic to guard against anger. Sir William Osler echoed this belief nineteen centuries later with the comment 'fright or violent emotion of any sort may bring on a paroxysm', and in his textbook of medicine stated, 'All writers agree that there is, in a majority of cases of bronchial asthma, a strong neurotic element.'

There was a flowering in the 1920s of interest in the ways in which psychological forces could induce and perpetuate bodily illness. Yet in the past three decades the study of allergic mechanisms in asthma has all but eclipsed any consideration of emotional influences. A recent huge tome on bronchial asthma devoted over 300 pages to allergy, yet dismissed psychological factors in just forty.

John Mackenzie, an ear, nose, and throat surgeon of Baltimore, writing in 1885 described a woman with summer seasonal hayfever and asthma, ascribed, as it often was, to the scent of roses. 'Mrs— thirty two years of age, in excellent circumstances, surrounded by all the comforts of life; very stout, well nourished, but physically weak. . .' Her asthma had begun at the age of twelve years, was summer seasonal and associated with typical itching of the nose and paroxysms of sneezing. Attacks of wheezing could be provoked by innumerable circumstances which included the odour of hay and roses. Mackenzie writes on: 'Decidedly sceptical as to the power of pollen to produce a paroxysm in her particular case, I practised the following deception upon her . . . I obtained an artificial rose of such exquisite workmanship that it presented a perfect counterfeit of the original.' During an interview 'I produced the artificial rose . . . and, sitting before her, held it in my hand, at the same time continuing the conversation. In the course of a minute she said she felt that she must sneeze . . . The nasal passages became suddenly obstructed . . . In a few minutes the feeling of oppression in the chest began, with slight embarassment of respiration.' It caused her great amazement to learn that the rose was artificial but the effect was wholly beneficial. A few days later she reported that she had buried her nostrils in a large fragrant specimen of the genuine article without the slightest ill effect.

This story is probably an example of conditioning. Allergy had not been clearly defined in 1885. Yet it must be supposed that the lady's asthma had been initiated by allergy to pollen. On this background a psychological mechanism operated. Her fear of developing wheezing on contact with roses was sufficient to cause her in fact to wheeze even though the rose was artificial.

Attempts have been made to reproduce this under more carefully controlled conditions. Two asthmatic women known to be sensitive to pollen were repeatedly tested with inhalations of pollen extract and an inert solution containing no pollen. At first they regularly developed wheeze with the pollen but were uninfluenced by the inert solution. They were not told which solution to expect. After several days of testing, they began to react to the inert solution as well as to the pollen. Next, wheezing was detectable when air alone was blown at them with no solution at all. Finally, the mere act of putting on the mouthpiece to start the test was sufficient to set off a reaction.

It is unfortunate that the assessment of wheezing in these studies depended on spirometric tests which can be influenced by motivation. One wonders what was so special about these two asthmatics and in how many others such an effect could have been produced. The experiments lack, too, some of the sophistication put into conditioning studies now. Yet if nothing else, these two women did reveal the power suggestion has on the airways.

Some of the most scientifically controlled studies of the influence of suggestion on asthma were carried out in the late 1960s by Luparello and his colleagues. Forty asthmatics allowed themselves to be subjected to a number of studies in which their lung function was assessed by techniques not dependent on co-operation or motivation. Measurements were made before and for four hours after the inhalation of an aerosol, which was simply a dilute solution of salt. The patients were told however that it was an allergen to which they knew they were sensitive. In almost half these asthmatics there was evidence of increased narrowing of the airways and in a quarter there was an obvious attack of asthma. In those who wheezed, a second inhalation of the same salt aerosol was given. This time they were told it was a treatment which would relax their airways. It did. Nothing quite matching these studies has been attempted since, though under hypnosis, a very special state of heightened suggestibility, the airways can be made to dilate or constrict by suggestion alone.

Emotion and Personality

The use of suggestion and hypnosis therapeutically is the logical outcome of these observations and the degree to which they have been successful we will judge later. An effect attributable to suggestion alone is an important facet to the assessment of new drug therapies in asthma. The active drug must always be checked against an inert 'placebo' preparation. In children for example some protection against wheezing after exercise can be obtained in 40 per cent by the use of a placebo.

The production of asthma by images of potentially allergic stimuli is one facet to the interaction between psychological forces and asthma. Another is the direct provocation of wheezing by psychological stress. Careful questioning of unselected asthmatics reveals that they often feel that their emotional state influences their asthma. Dr Storr described on page 4 how, in him, undue stress provoked asthma. Many patients would echo his experience. The range of emotions implicated is wide—anger, anxiety, depression, guilt, even pleasurable excitement and joy. The triggering of attacks of wheezing by emotional stress can be recorded in up to 70 per cent of asthmatics: but it is very rarely the only trigger. Indeed, it is perhaps the interaction between emotional and non-emotional factors that is of most interest.

This is revealed in an anecdote told by Trousseau, a notable nineteenth century French physician, about himself. He was an asthmatic. His worst attack of asthma occurred in a grain loft. The air was dusty but on this occasion there was an emotional charge in the atmosphere. Trousseau suspected his coachman of dishonesty in measuring the oats, and had decided on this occasion to supervise the operation. 'I had a hundred times been exposed to an atmosphere of dust considerably thicker . . . (This time it) acted on me whilst I was in a peculiar state. My nervous system was shaken from the influence of mental emotion caused by the idea of a theft, however trifling, committed by one of my servants.'

This type of interaction between emotional and allergic stimuli is potentially more relevant to the everyday life of the asthmatic. It has been studied objectively. A small dose of pollen extract was released into the atmosphere unbeknown to the patient and insufficient to cause any wheezing. An interviewer then discussed various aspects of that patient's asthma with him. If the discussion touched on unpleasant circumstances associated with his asthma, then wheezing was provoked; if these topics were avoided there was no wheezing.

Whilst some anomalies are encountered in relating emotional stress to wheezing—such as why stress can both heighten and relieve wheezing —there is no difficulty in proposing ways in which psychological events might influence the airways. Higher centres in the brain can cause the airways to contract through the parasympathetic nervous system. Indeed, medicines which antagonize parasympathetic nerve activity partly ameliorate the adverse effects of suggestion on the airways. Conversely, stress activates the adrenal glands to secrete hormones which can relax bronchial muscle. There is some suggestion that this response is less vigorous in the asthmatic than in healthy subjects.

A further case history will serve to underline points already made in relation to suggestion and conditioning, and introduce another facet into this narrative. An asthmatic Dutch woman known to be allergic to pollens and house dust believed herself to be allergic to goldfish. This seemed strange since there was no way in which the goldfish could give off any allergens that could be inhaled. Under circumstances where lung function tests could be carried out, she was shown a live goldfish in a bowl. She became wheezy. On a second occasion she was shown a toy goldfish in a bowl. Despite the fact that she realized it was ridiculous, she again became wheezy. Finally she became wheezy when shown an empty goldfish bowl.

During the course of these tests she had a dream. In her dream she saw a huge goldfish bowl. On a shelf high above it were her books. She wanted to read why goldfishes cause asthma. She climbed on a chair and reached for the book, but it was too high. She lost her balance and fell into the goldfish bowl. The fishes swam around. She gasped for breath. Her neck became caught in a strand of water weed. Suddenly she was awake, wheezing, and fighting for breath.

This patient described too, how when she was a child, her mother had thrown away her goldfish, which she had loved much, and saved her pocket money to buy. The memories became all too real, when in an attempt to stop her wheezing in the final study the experimenter smashed the goldfish bowl. The wheezing intensified. 'That is exactly what my mother did,' she exclaimed. 'She threw the bowl into the dustbin.'

The implication from this account is that tension between the asthmatic and her mother was in some way responsible for the child's asthma. Various aspects of the parent/child relationship have been thought to be significant perpetuating factors in childhood asthma. The removal of an asthmatic child from home to hospital is often accompanied by immediate and dramatic improvement. The change seems disproportionate to the effect that might be expected for removal from environmental allergens. Cats, dogs, and household dust may be important triggers but there is a suggestion that they act on a background of psychological stress.

PLATE I

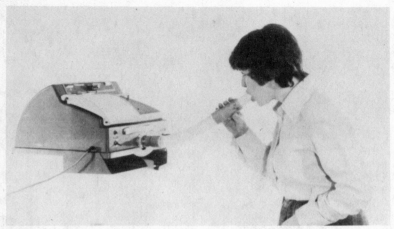

(a) A dry bellows spirometer. (By kind permission of Vitalograph Ltd.)

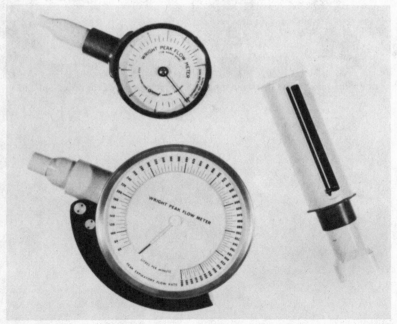

(b) Three versions of the Wright Peak Flow Meter – paediatric (top left), adult (bottom left), portable mini-flow meter (right). (By kind permission of Airmed Ltd.)

PLATE II

Patient having lung function tests in a body plethysmograph. (Fenyves & Gut Ltd.)

PLATE III

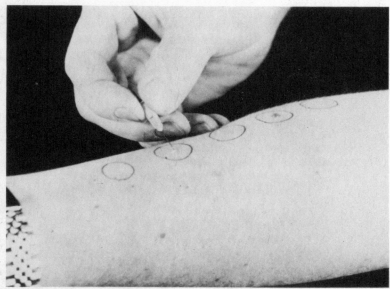

(a) Prick test being performed by picking up the superficial layers of the skin through a drop of allergen.

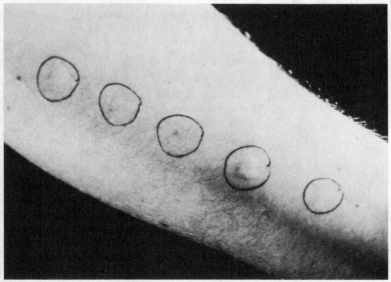

(b) Positive skin prick test weals.

PLATE IV

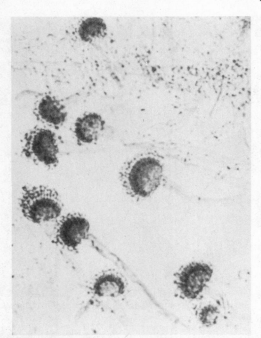

(a) Spores of the mould Aspergillus fumigatus. (By kind permission of Dr. R. Davies, St. Mary's Hospital.)

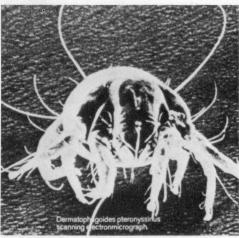

(b) A house-dust mite as viewed with the electron microscope. (By kind permission of Bencard.)

PLATE V

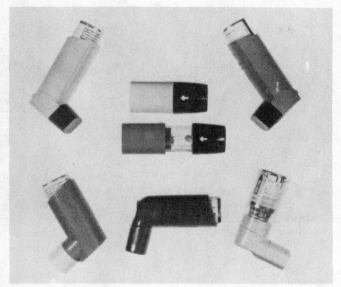

(a) Five pressurized aerosols used for delivering bronchodilators and (top centre) a Rotahaler.

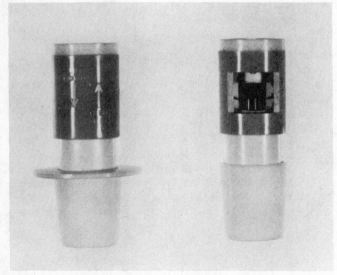

(b) The Spinhaler: for administering DSCG (Intal). The capsule is placed inside the device and punctured using the prongs illustrated in the cut-away inhaler on the right. The one on the left is the more recently introduced version with a cuff on the mouthpiece.

PLATE VI

Patient using a portable Bennet machine for delivery of a bronchodilator aerosol. (By kind permission of the manufacturers.)

PLATE VII

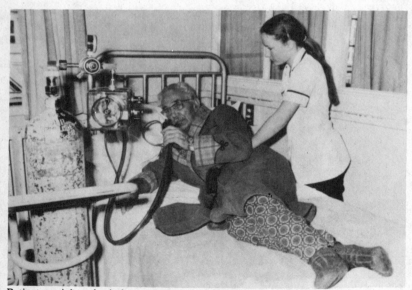

Patient receiving physiotherapy together with positive pressure breathing from a Bird machine. (By kind permission of the manufacturers.)

Emotion and Personality

When asthmatic Dutch children were sent to Switzerland during World War II they were certainly being removed from the influence of the house dust mite. This creature survives poorly in the dry heights of the Alps. The children improved: and they did rather better than local Swiss asthmatic children. After the war, a residential school for asthmatics was set up in Holland itself. The Dutch children showed just as much improvement in their asthma when in the Dutch school as they did in Switzerland. The Dutch residential school had as many mites as the children's own homes. The common feature between the residential schools was not removal from household allergens, but the separation of the children from their parents.

In Denver, Colorado, in the USA, a residential home has been run since the 1930s for children with chronic severe asthma. They remain there from one to three years. As few as one in twenty fail to benefit from their stay. On returning to their own homes, half of these children require no treatment, and the remainder manage well on reduced treatment. That the separation of the children from their parents is critical in this exercise is made clear from a reversal of the usual separation procedure. Instead of removing the child to a residential home, the parents were moved into a hotel and appropriate provisions made for the children in their own homes. For those children in whom family tensions were felt to be important, the results were beneficial.

The root of the tension in these children often lies in the overprotective attitude of their parents. It is distressing to see a child with acute asthma. It is natural for parents to do all they can to protect their children from environmental allergens, from 'catching cold', from the mockery of school fellows: but it can be carried too far. One of the benefits that follow removing a child to hospital may be the stimulus it gives to the child to become independent from an understandable but stifling attitude by his parents.

Other features of living at home which seem to be associated with recurrent severe asthma are quite the reverse and stem from deprivation. Neglect caused by poverty and overcrowding, marital disharmony, parental separation, the death of a parent, are all mentioned. None are specific causes for asthma. But they are all potentially serious for the child with irritable asthmatic airways.

These observations leave little doubt that in some childhood asthmatics, there is a sufficient background of tension in the home to make this a significant factor in the persistence of the child's asthma. But how often does this happen? The Denver physician states, 'I selected only the sickest for admission in the home.' There is no satisfactory

71

information on which to base a reliable estimate. About a quarter of the children attending an asthma clinic at a London teaching hospital were described as having severe perennial asthma. These would be the type of patients from whom the Denver children were selected. But since only about one in five of childhood asthmatics attends a hospital clinic, the number who might be suffering in this way is likely to be well under 5 per cent.

Set against this small minority of childhood asthmatics is the vast majority in whom emotional tensions play a minor or insignificant role. The excitement of parties or holidays may bubble over into wheezing and not infrequently there is an element of manipulation perhaps for example in relation to examinations. Yet in general the attitude of children is more one of domination over, rather than domination by, their asthma.

It has been suggested that if asthma can be influenced by psychological events, asthmatics ought to have a readily identifiable personality. Analyses of the personality traits of asthmatics are legion. Asthmatics have been described as irritable, easily aroused to anger, whining, complaining. They have been categorized as obsessional neurotics. They have been seen as lacking self-confidence and frequently depressed.

Defects exist in many of the studies making it difficult to interpret the findings. Inappropriate questions have been asked or inadequate control studies carried out. Overall, there seems to be no clearcut evidence that there is a specific asthmatic personality. Perhaps it is fair to comment on some of the better studies to illustrate the extremes of opinion.

Those who most strongly support the concept of a specific asthmatic personality are the psychoanalysts. They start with the asthmatic's frequently voiced opinions of himself: 'I don't show my feelings easily': 'I bottle things up'. The free expression of emotion brings relief. To inhibit emotional expression invites tension. The postulate is that in the asthmatic, the tension is reflected in the lungs. This conversion of emotional tensions into a bodily disorder makes the conflict more socially acceptable. Even today the sight of an asthmatic wheezing engenders more pity than does overt neurotic disturbance. The suppressed emotion is generally not consciously appreciated. If it can be revealed and the tension broken, the asthma may clear. This has been described. A young woman, asthmatic since childhood, recalled under psychoanalysis a scene from her childhood in which someone had been strangled. Her fear had been suppressed and, with it, her memory of the event, but she became asthmatic. Treatment enabled her to resolve her fears and her asthma disappeared.

Emotion and Personality

Children occasionally seem to be able to manipulate their asthma consciously. 'I think myself into an attack.' Indeed whether consciously recognized or not, it is in childhood emotional conflicts that the psychoanalysts find most support for their theories. The most specifically enunciated conflict related to asthma is that it is a form of 'suppressed crying'. Here we have the disturbed parent/child relationship again. The child loves his mother intensely yet feels her rejecting him. Crying would alienate the mother further, but its conversion into asthmatic wheezing calls forth her pity and love. Anecdotal support is easy to find amongst the famous. Marcel Proust was pathologically attached to his beloved 'Mamma'. Yet he frequently quarrelled with her, and suffered many bouts of wheezing as a result. In his youth, Theodore Roosevelt was asthmatic and clearly very close to his mother. When aged eleven he wrote, 'I was very sick last night and Mamma was so very kind telling me storrys (sic) and rubbing me with her delicate fingers.' Throwing off his dependence in his teens, Roosevelt's asthma ceased to bother him seriously.

This firm confidence in a specific type of emotional conflict being responsible for asthma is not widely shared. It has been pointed out that many surveys have suggested that asthmatics are unduly neurotic, anxiety-prone, and obsessional. Two reservations make the validity of these comments suspect. The first is illustrated by a comparative study from Edinburgh. In this, the asthmatics were compared with a control population which included those who were in robust mental health and those who were frankly neurotic. The degree of neuroticism elicited amongst the asthmatics was halfway between the two extremes: and so was the average of the control population as a whole. In other words, asthmatics are a bit neurotic. But so are we all!

The second reservation arises from studies in which asthmatics have been compared with those having other types of physical handicap. The asthmatics appeared no more anxious, nor neurotically disturbed in any specific way than others with a physical disability. This raises the classic hen and egg argument. Did the anxious personality precede the development of the asthma and perhaps in some way contribute towards it? Or did it arise as a result of constant fear of another attack and anxiety over school or work prospects?

There can be no specific answer to these questions nor any definitive assessment of the role of psychogenic factors in asthma. None would argue with the view that anxiety and stress may trigger an attack in an established asthmatic. Most physicians know of patients in whom psychogenic factors have seemed to be responsible for the initiation of a spell of asthma, or have contributed to the perpetuation of asthma once established. But few would regard this as common and would not concur with the view that there is a specific personality type universally encountered in asthmatic patients.

Finally it must be remembered that breathlessness itself carries psychological overtones. The difficulty in drawing breath whether experienced or anticipated can itself engender a state of tension that will intensify any distress directly attributed to the airways narrowing.

7

Age and inheritance

PREVIOUS chapters have given a description of airways irritability and of the three major trigger factors for attacks of asthma—allergy, infection, and emotion—which has created a picture of asthma in individuals. These miniature portraits need to be collected together on a broader canvas. The scene that emerges has certain themes. These relate to the temporal pattern of attacks of asthma, the balance of trigger factors, and the changing face asthma presents at different ages.

Asthma is by definition and by its very nature, an intermittent disorder. The asthmatic's irritable airways respond to fumes, to laughter, to exercise, with a brief spasm of wheezing that passes off almost as readily as it came. Between such episodes, though the potential for becoming wheezy remains, the airways are clear. The asthmatic sensitive to cats, or horse hair, or pollen will wheeze when these allergens are in the air he breathes: but at other times his airways, unmolested, cause him no distress. An attack of wheezy bronchitis may carry in its train several days, or even a couple of weeks, of shortness of breath but, with treatment, it all recovers and once more the asthmatic breathes freely. Stress or anxiety will heighten wheeziness for a while but with the easing of tension or the acceptance of disappointment, the airways relax again. All these are commonplace facets of asthma as it is experienced by the great majority of asthmatics. Their asthma is intermittent: between attacks they are completely free of wheezing.

A pattern of intermittent attacks is not only the common way that asthma presents, it is the least serious. At all ages those with intermittent attacks are most likely to remain in good health, to be minimally bothered by asthma, or to lose their asthma altogether. When Ogilvie reviewed, after an average of eleven years, 1000 patients with asthma seen personally by him, two-thirds of those who had presented with intermittent asthma had been either free of asthma for two years or had had no more than seven days disability each year.

Age and inheritance

Intermittent asthma may be contrasted with the pattern of asthma in those who have some degree of shortness of breath between attacks. There is no clear demarcation between those having very severe sharp attacks with some wheeziness between, and those with virtually constant disabling shortness of breath on top of which some variability is superimposed. This more persistent asthma is given various labels. Some, like Ogilvie, call it 'continuous', others 'persistent' asthma. Yet others would use the term chronic asthma. 'Chronic' describes correctly symptoms that persist over many weeks, months, or even years. It carries an implication of constant ill-health or even slow deterioration that belies the degree of reversibility that is potentially always possible in asthma. In medicine the contrast to 'chronic', is 'acute'. Each individual attack of asthma may have an acute or sudden onset, but it is not usual to describe the general pattern of intermittent asthma as acute.

Continuous asthma contrasts with intermittent asthma in several respects. Not least amongst these is the poorer outlook with which it is associated. Ogilvie's asthmatics who presented with continuous asthma stood only a one-in-three chance of being in good health after eleven years, compared with the two-in-three chance of those with intermittent asthma. The drawing of this contrast between intermittent and continuous asthmatic symptoms helped Ogilvie to highlight two broad patterns amongst his population of asthmatics, who attended hospital. They relate to the trigger factors for the asthma, and the age of onset of the asthma. Briefly, for these points will come up again, it emerges first that intermittent asthma is rather unlikely to be associated with bronchitis, and secondly that four out of every five of those with intermittent asthma had begun to wheeze before the age of 16 (Fig. 14).

Whilst this review of asthma by Ogilvie was based on a division by the clinical pattern of attacks, others have used a division based on 'cause'. The best-known analysis along these lines is that of Rackemann who described his asthmatic patients as either having 'extrinsic' or 'intrinsic' asthma. In extrinsic asthma 'the attacks are due to contact with foreign substances in the environment outside the body': this is thus virtually synonymous with asthma due to allergy. With intrinsic asthma the cause was believed to lie somehow within the patient. It was, at least initially, thought by Rackemann to be a specific reactivity to infection. In such patients cutaneous prick tests for atopic allergy were negative, whereas they were positive in the extrinsic group. The difficulty with such a distinction, drawn on the grounds of demonstrating specific allergies, was, and always will be, that one can never be

Age and inheritance

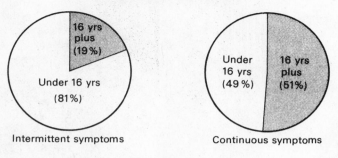

Fig. 14. Age of onset of asthma in relation to intermittent or continuous symptoms. (Data of Dr A. G. Ogilvie: *Thorax*, 1962).

certain that all allergens have been tested for. The contrast drawn between extrinsic and intrinsic asthma does somewhat follow the clinical pattern of intermittent versus continuous asthma, but not closely. Extrinsic asthma is often intermittent, but quite often allergic factors are found in those with continuous symptoms. The age feature crops up again: Rackemann writes: 'When asthma begins before age thirty, the cause is allergy unless proved otherwise: but when asthma begins after age forty, the cause is not allergy unless proved otherwise.' Such broad generalizations, whilst subject to many individual exceptions, help to create an overall picture of asthma.

The term intrinsic asthma has been subjected to many nuances of meaning since its introduction. It has been used when no specific cause could be found for the asthma. It has been regarded as synonymous with infection causing asthma. In the absence of external environmental allergens, infection is certainly a frequent trigger but even so it is not the underlying cause for the asthma. Intrinsic has been applied to the condition of patients with continuous asthma where a whole variety of factors may precipitate wheezing. In view of these complexities it may be that the term should be abandoned.

To draw a clear distinction between extrinsic and intrinsic, allergic and non-allergic asthma is almost certainly too simplistic. Though allergy is a common trigger it is rarely the only cause of wheezing in an individual. Infections are seldom singled out by patients as the sole occasions on which they wheeze. It is likewise with emotional stress. In nearly 500 asthmatics of all ages examined in Cardiff, infective factors seemed to trigger asthma in 88 per cent, psychological factors in 70 per cent, and allergic factors in 64 per cent. All three operated

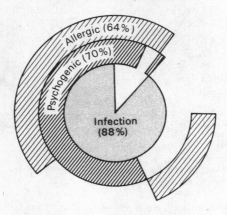

Fig. 15. Reported influence of allergic, psychogenic, and infective factors in triggering attacks of asthma.

together in 38 per cent. However, infection was the sole cause of asthma in only 11 per cent, allergy in only 3 per cent and psychological stress in only 1 per cent. So whilst in an individual one factor may be a frequent trigger, others nearly always play their part, and it is often a constellation of circumstances which sets off an asthmatic attack.

Asthma emerges from any analysis such as this, not as a specific condition with a specific cause, but rather as a disturbance of the behaviour of the airways. They are irritable. It is not a feature of healthy airways to tighten up when there is a chance breathing in of cold air. A few pollen grains or some specks of household dust are harmless except to the sensitive asthmatic. Bronchitis is a common ailment: it is not normally accompanied by wheezing except in the asthmatic. Emotional stress is an accepted hazard of life: only in the asthmatic does it cause the airways to narrow. The environmental irritants, allergens, infections, and stresses which assail the asthmatic differ in no way from those the rest of us experience. It is in their impact on the way in which the airways function that the difference lies. Indeed it is the very irritability of the airways that would seem to be the underlying defect.

Rackemann's contention that intrinsic asthma is due to an underlying constitutional defect can be enlarged to embrace a view that in all asthma there is an underlying defect on top of which various triggers act. Allergy seems to be an important trigger in some, infection in others, emotion in others, and in most, more than one trigger operates.

Age and inheritance

The underlying defect would seem most likely to be the undue tendency of the asthmatic's airways to narrow in response to all manner of irritants—whether these be specific allergens, chemicals or non-specific dusts and fumes.

In all population studies of asthma there emerges a very distinctive pattern in relation to age. Asthma starts and is most commonly seen at two phases of life—childhood and middle age. A chronological look at asthma at different ages is both interesting and instructive.

Childhood asthma

Asthma is common in children. In England and Wales there are perhaps half a million children with this condition. It is indeed the commonest chronic disease of childhood (Fig. 16). Despite this, most children do not have troublesome asthma and in only a few can it be described as severe.

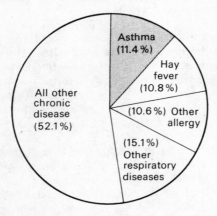

Fig. 16. Chronic diseases in children (Data from US National Health Survey, 1959–61).

One of the most remarkable and unexplained facts about childhood asthma is the predilection it has for boys. In every study boys outnumber girls by an average of over two to one. This excess of boys over girls is more obvious in younger children as can be seen from the chart depicting sex ratio against age (Fig. 17). Boys particularly predominate over girls in the more severe grades of asthma.

As at other ages, asthma in children presents for the most part a

79

Age and inheritance

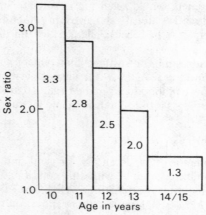

Fig. 17. Sex ratio of boys to girls at various ages (Based on data from Dr B. Dawson and co-workers, *Lancet*, 1969).

pattern of episodic wheezing. Infection and exercise are the precipitants most commonly described by asthmatic children. Three quarters of all asthmatic children suffer no more than infrequent mild attacks of wheezing with long free intervals between them. They cause no real disturbances to daily life and are easily treated with simple remedies. In schoolchildren from Melbourne, Australia, it was found that over half the asthmatics had had a total of less than ten attacks of asthma by the age of ten years.

How else does asthma first make itself evident in children? It not infrequently presents as coughing alone without any wheezing being obvious. Because of this, thoughts will not immediately turn to asthma, but a careful analysis of the circumstances under which the coughing occurs will reveal that it follows the same pattern as that described for wheezing. Thus the coughing will be most obvious during the night, on awakening in the morning and after exercise.

Asthma may develop quite gradually on top of a story of essentially nasal symptons. These children have what seems to be recurrent head colds with a running and then a blocked nose. They are dubbed 'catarrhal'. Wheezing appears without an obvious trigger, perhaps first at night, or after exertion. The asthma is not severe, just intermittently bothersome. There is a no story of bronchitis and there are no other features pointing to infection.

It is tempting to suppose that many of the features of childhood

80

asthma are due to allergy, but an attempt to tie up symptoms with exposure to some agent likely to cause allergy, generally fails. Indeed, asthma in children which is unequivocally and solely allergically precipitated is quite uncommon. There are individual children who only get asthma after contact with a horse, a cat, or a dog: but these are a minority. Asthma during the pollen season is a somewhat separate problem occurring in rather older children and will be considered later.

Though asthma in children may not often be due exclusively to allergy, yet a close and fundamental relationship exists between atopic allergy and childhood asthma. There is a striking concurrence of infantile eczema and rhinitis with asthma in certain young children. The eczema comes on in the first year of life: perhaps it is only in the creases of the elbows and behind the knees, or the wrists, hands, trunk, and face may be affected as well. Persistent 'colds' afflict the child's nose and by the age of two years he has usually had his first attack of wheezing. The asthma is well established by the age of five years. Attacks at night are common. Others last days and leave the child exhausted. There may be a clearing of the eczema with each attack of asthma. Between attacks, symptoms settle slowly. It is these children that make up the majority of those who go on to have persistent symptoms. Indeed two thirds of children with frequent persistent asthma have or have had eczema: and over 90 per cent of them show positive skin tests of the atopic type.

Atopic allergy and asthma march closer together in childhood than at any other age. Despite this, allergy alone cannot explain all the vagaries of behaviour in the asthmatic child. What allergy can induce wheezing after laughter or exercise? Are the emotions allergic? And what of the many children who show positive skin tests but who have no asthma? For every atopic child with asthma, there are three who are atopic but do not have asthma. The atopic state can clearly exist without asthma. Is the reverse true? Not very often in children. Only seven per cent of the Melbourne children with severe asthma never had positive skin prick tests at any stage during the fourteen years of the survey. However about half of those with mild or infrequent asthma were always skin test negative. It looks as though in most instances the irritability factor, best exemplified by exercise-induced asthma, must interact with atopic allergy, best exemplified by positive skin tests, before asthma can develop. Despite this a very few asthmatic children do not have exercise-induced asthma and a very few do not have positive skin tests. Whether asthma can occur if neither of these is present is not clear.

Age and inheritance

If asthma is going to develop in childhood it is likely to do so early on. More than half will have had their first wheezing attack before three years of age: and only about 10 per cent of childhood asthmatics first wheeze after the age of five. If they do so they are likely to have mild asthma and to experience few attacks. It is the children who develop asthma in infancy who are likely to have both a greater severity and a greater likelihood of persisting symptoms at the age of ten years.

	Onset	Cessation
Mild asthma	78% start after 2 yrs 64% start after 3 yrs	80% stop before 8 yrs 89% stop before 10 yrs
Moderate asthma	59% start after 2 yrs 31% start after 3 yrs	46% stop before 8 yrs 68% stop before 10 yrs
Severe asthma	49% start after 2 yrs 28% start after 3 yrs	None stop before 10 yrs

Fig. 18. The relation of severity to age of onset and cessation of asthma in Australian children. (Based on data of Drs K. McNicol and H. W. Williams, *British Medical Journal*, 1973).

The tale that children 'grow out' of asthma is not a myth. By ten, nearly two thirds of children can be expected to be free of wheezing and by adolescence over 80 per cent. Those left wheezing at this age are the children with persistent and bothersome symptoms throughout childhood. These children are likely to have fallen behind their peers in height and weight. They are more likely to have developed chest deformities as a result of chronically overinflated chests.

If children with asthma are monitored throughout childhood, the number giving positive prick tests increases, even though the extent to which they are bothered by asthma lessens. Hayfever symptoms also become more common early in the second decade of life. Hayfever beginning for the first time in an atopic child who has not previously had asthma is likely to do so in the early teenage years. Pollen asthma may accompany the hayfever as noted earlier. When it does, the asthma is often purely summer seasonal. Even so, it does not behave in an exclusively 'allergic' way. Whilst the hayfever may come on immediately after exposure to pollen, the asthma rarely does. More often it appears

82

Age and inheritance

in the familiar form of nocturnal wheezing attacks. As the season advances, the wheezing persists into the day, but exacerbations in a pollen-laden atmosphere are not prominent. Exercise, cold air, and irritant dusts may now set off wheezing, whereas in the winter these can be tolerated without ill effect. The pollen is clearly an essential factor in the development of the asthma, but it creates a state in which many triggers, not just allergy, will set up wheezing.

Hayfever and pollen asthma tend to be less and less bothersome by the late teenage years. Most other childhood asthmatics have 'grown out' of their asthma by this age. So, early adult life tends to be a period of life when asthma is less common. Those bothered by asthma at this stage include children whose symptoms have persisted through the teenage years and the few whose asthma begins for the first time at this age.

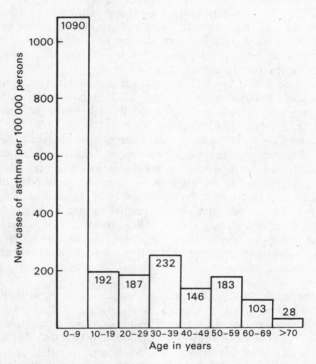

Fig. 19. Incidence of asthma per 100 000 persons in relation to age of onset. (Based on data from Dr E. H. Derrick, *Medical Journal of Australia*, 1971).

83

Age and inheritance

Adult asthma

The factors associated with onset of asthma in early adult life are quite variable. As at other stages allergy, infection, and stress may be implicated. An important minority will have asthma that is specifically related to their working environment. These occupational asthmas are sufficiently important to warrant a chapter to themselves (p. 92).

In women, asthma may begin for the first time just after childbirth. In those previously bothered by asthma, pregnancy seems to have a totally unpredictable effect. The asthma may improve. If so, this is generally obvious quite early in pregnancy. In some it may deteriorate: this is more likely later in pregnancy. The physical encumbrance of the growing child may be responsible, but so might hormonal changes. The pattern of hormonal changes in pregnancy is reflected in those of the menstrual cycle. In women with pre-existing asthma, the asthma may improve early in the menstrual cycle and deteriorate during the later part of the cycle. It may also first become obvious about the time of the menopause. How these presumed hormonal factors influence the onset or expression of asthma is now known.

As middle life is reached there is an increase in the amount of asthma seen. Asthmatics at this age fall into two broad categories. Those previously atopic as children and those in whom asthma begins for the first time in middle life.

The previous atopic history in these adults is sometimes no more than a little eczema or teenage hayfever without asthma. But many wheezed or had frank asthma at some stage in childhood. They then became symptom free in early adult life. The recurrence of their asthma may at first mimic the childhood pattern, say with some hayfever, but it soon becomes a more general asthma with attacks triggered by a variety of agents. Of the triggers of asthma in adult life, infection seems to play an increasing part. This is true to an extent of adult asthmatics who are atopic. It is even more characteristic of the non-atopic adults in whom asthma becomes manifest for the first time.

In the adult, chest infections are associated both with the first attack of asthma (or its re-appearance after years of absence) and with recurring attacks. An appreciable number of these asthmatics do not give positive skin prick tests for atopic allergy and thus fall into the group usually classified as 'intrinsic'. The story is often one of persistent coughing and wheezing initiated by an influenzal illness. Several courses of antibiotics may be given with disappointing results. The

Age and inheritance

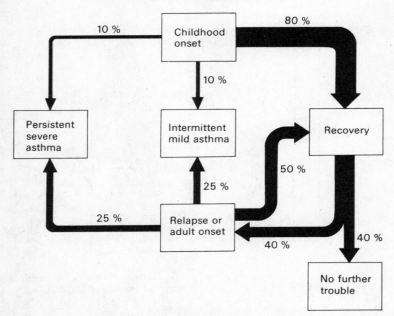

Fig. 20. A general scheme illustrating the outcome of asthma: very approximate figures on several series from different countries.

illness does not respond until it is appreciated that there is a wheezy component and appropriate treatment prescribed. The same sequence follows another infection months later. The interval between infective wheezy episodes may shorten but this is not predictable. There may be persisting shortness of breath between attacks with weather conditions appearing to be responsible for episodic chest tightness. Progression to a state of chronic disability occurs more frequently at this age than in childhood. In the Newcastle patients followed up by Ogilvie, only 20 per cent of those who had developed bronchitis were in good health at follow-up compared with a record of good health in 92 per cent of those who had not developed bronchitis (Fig. 21). Most researchers are however at pains to point out that this applies only to the development of wheezy bronchitis in the adult. As previously indicated episodic wheezy bronchitis in children carries a relatively good prognosis.

Wheezing in the adult all too often presents a difficult diagnostic dilemma between asthma and chronic bronchitis. The latter condition,

Age and inheritance

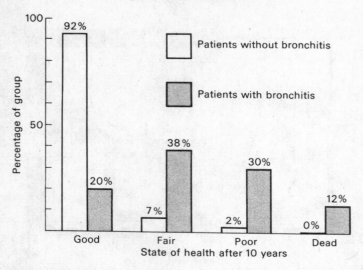

Fig. 21. The effect of the development of bronchitis on the state of health of adult asthmatics followed up after ten years. (Based on data of Dr A. G. Ogilvie, *Thorax* 1962).

it will be recalled from Chapter 1, is due to smoking. Some chronic bronchitics develop narrowed airways. This narrowing is more permanent and progressive than that seen in asthma, but in some adults it is, at least initially, quite remarkably reversible.Infection is an important trigger for episodes of reversible wheeziness in the adult smoker. In these, the wheezy bronchitis has many parallels to the wheezy bronchitis seen in asthmatics. Why some smokers develop wheezing and not others is a mystery. One important clue is that adults who smoke and who become disabled by breathlessness are more likely to have had some sort of childhood respiratory illness. The survey which reported these findings depended on the adults searching back in their memories to recall details of what happened to them as children. The information thus cannot be wholly reliable and any distinction between different sorts of childhood respiratory illness, wheezy bronchitis, cough, asthma, or other conditions such as pneumonia or tuberculosis was not possible. Nonetheless in a fair proportion, the childhood illness must have been asthma or wheezy bronchitis. It is possible then to argue either that smoking is one of the factors likely to trigger asthma in those constitutionally predisposed to it, or that in smokers a previous history of asthma makes them more prone to the injurious effects of tobacco smoke.

Besides infection, many adults rank stress as important in initiating or reactivating their asthma. Earning a living becomes more physically arduous. Family life brings its worries. The realities of life demand that ideals be compromised for practicalities. Some record that it is not the stress itself but the relief from tension that comes after a particularly stressful time has passed, that initiates the asthma. A woman may develop wheezing after nursing her husband through a terminal illness. A man finds his job increasingly demanding yet is resentful when he is passed over for promotion: he too may become asthmatic. Individual case records can be very convincing. How specific these psychological stresses are in initiating asthma in the adult is debatable and how they interact with other internal or external factors to trigger asthma is unknown. Periods of anxiety are not rare and it is tempting to attribute physical illness to stress.

It is uncommon for asthma to appear for the first time in the elderly. Unless they have previously been known to have asthma, wheezing shortness-of-breath in those over sixty-five is more likely to be due to the effects of smoking or to some other chest or heart condition. When asthma does have an onset at such a late age, infection is very likely to be a factor in both initiating the illness and in triggering subsequent attacks. Persistent symptoms, with a need for continuous medication and a progressive course are the rule.

Inheritance

Those with asthma often ask whether they are likely to pass the disorder on to their children. There is no simple answer to this question. There is no doubt that asthma 'runs in families'. Sennertus described it in three successive generations of his wife's family in 1650. Deciding exactly how it is inherited or what chance there is that a given individual will develop asthma, is difficult.

In 1864 H. H. Salter wrote 'with regard to the inheritance of asthma, I have observed one curious fact . . . several brothers and sisters in a family may be asthmatic without the parents having been so. This would seem to suggest . . . that certain combinations . . . lead to the creation of certain peculiarities, and that the qualities of progeny are not the mere results of the combined qualities of the parents.' This degree of insight was remarkable considering the date. The horticultural studies that were to lay the cornerstone on which an understanding of inheritance could be built had not yet been published.

Our modern understanding of genetics began with Gregor Mendel, born into a poor Austrian peasant family in 1822. He became a priest, and in 1858, abbot of the monastery at Brno in present day Czechoslovakia. There, he carried out his painstaking crossbreeding experiments with the garden pea. They revealed that some characteristics were dominant, appearing in the offspring whether they received the genetic signal from both or from just one parent. Other characteristics were recessive and appeared only when inherited from both parents. Such simple rules explained the inheritance of eye colour, and in animals fur colour. For other characteristics, such as height or blood pressure, several different genetic signals seemed to be necessary, since the inheritance could not be explained by applying simple Mendelian rules.

How do the rules work in asthma? Certainly not in a simple way. The first large-scale surveys carried out in the second decade of this century showed that in about half of any group of allergic patients there was a family history of allergy. This allergy included not only asthma but other conditions. Some, like infantile eczema and hayfever, were firmly atopic, but others were of dubious origin and would not today be classed as allergic. It did seem that if two parents were allergic their children had a good change of developing an allergic disorder before the age of puberty. With one parent affected the children might develop allergy later in life. If neither was allergic, then the children were unlikely to be so. The conclusion was drawn that it was 'the tendency to develop allergy' that is inherited.

Not a great deal of evidence was added which could identify this tendency further for the next thirty or forty years. More recently two approaches have helped to clarify the situation. First a large number of twins with asthma have been studied; secondly family studies have been conducted with more precision, identifying not only asthma but also atopy.

Twin studies provide a valuable source of information for the study of inheritance. It must be accurately known if the twins are identical (both developing from a single fertilized egg), or non-identical (developing at the same time from two eggs separately fertilized). The distinction is easy if the non-identical twins are of different sex, but less so if of the same sex. If the tendency to asthma is inherited, then it should appear in both twins if they are identical, more frequently than in both non-identical twins. The largest study of this type comes from the Swedish twin registry. More than 7000 pairs of twins were questioned about asthma. Asthma appeared in both twins in nearly 20 per cent of identical twins, but in only a quarter as many of non-identical twins. This points to the inheritance of a tendency to asthma which requires for its expression some additional influence or else it would inevitably occur in both identical twins. This influence with identical twins must be external or environmental.

Reference has already been made to the close but not strictly parallel association between asthma and atopy (as assessed by skin prick tests). For example most children who are going to develop asthma have done so by the age of five. Yet the number of skin test positive children increases throughout childhood and reaches its peak in the teens. This divergence between asthma and atopy can be picked up in detailed family studies. Both atopic and non-atopic asthmatics show an increased family incidence of asthma. It is somewhat more marked in the atopic asthmatics. It seems that being atopic allows the underlying tendency to asthma to express itself more easily. Atopy is also inherited but not necessarily together with asthma. There is a hint that the inherited asthmatic trait is the irritable nature of the airways. Some relatives of asthmatics respond to exercise with airways narrowing in an asthmatic way even though they themselves have never wheezed.

A positive skin test is but a crude manifestation of allergic responsiveness. Serum antibody levels, especially of immunoglobulin E (IgE), are a more reliable index. It is now possible to analyse in great detail other markers of immunity. Results in asthma have been rather disappointing. This may well be because the situation is much more complex than is at present appreciated. Information from ragweed sensitive atopic asthmatics suggests that inherited characteristics determine the ease with which IgE antibody can be produced. If IgE production is damped down only a very powerful antigenic stimulus can break through to produce allergic symptoms. On the other hand if IgE forms more easily, less powerful antigens and more of them could produce symptoms.

Whatever the precise explanation, there is no doubt that some aspects of the tendency to asthma are inherited. Allergy and atopy seem to be inherited separately and, with environmental and perhaps psychological influences, determine the extent to which the inherited tendency to asthma is expressed. It is possible to gain some further insight into the relationship between inheritance and environment in asthma first by looking at certain occupational asthmas, and secondly by taking a worldwide view of asthma. This will be done in the next two chapters.

8

Asthma and occupation

THE first allusion to asthma as an occupational disease comes in the writings of Georgius Agricola over four hundred years ago: 'Some mines are so dry that . . . the dust which is stirred and beaten up by digging, penetrates into the windpipes and lungs, and produces difficulty in breathing and the disease which the Greeks called asthma.' Subsequent experience has taught that though miners certainly suffer breathing difficulties, this is rarely asthma as we understand it.

A century and a half later, occupational medicine was created almost overnight by the publication in 1700 of the book *De Morbus Artificum Diatribe*. It records the painstaking observations of one man, Bernadino Ramazzini of Modena. It is a classic. He enquired into the working conditions of potters, tinsmiths, tanners, cheesemakers, stonecutters, grooms, farmers, and countless others, and concluded: 'Medicine, like jurisprudence, should make a contribution to the wellbeing of workers and see to it that so far as possible, they should exercise their callings without harm.' He described for the first time many conditions caused directly or indirectly by working conditions. To doctors he left wise and treasured advice: 'When a doctor visits a working-class home he should be content to sit on a three-legged stool, if there isn't a gilded chair, and he should take time for his examination: and to the questions recommended by Hippocrates he should add one more—What is your occupation?'

Only some of the complaints described by Ramazzini were asthmatic. In the twentieth century the ever-increasing diversity of industrial processes using chemicals, creating vapours and raising dusts has vastly multiplied the opportunities for the lungs to react to inhaled agents by producing asthma. Even so, asthma related to occupation accounts for only two per cent of all asthma. Yet its importance far outstretches its numerical incidence. The detective work involved in tracking down the responsible agents is always fascinating. Fundamental questions about mechanisms are raised by studying the patterns of asthmatic symptoms. And the potential for cure exists by the use of simple techniques of industrial hygiene.

What clues should alert the physician to the possibility of occupational asthma? Asthma coming on for the first time in a working adult.

Asthma and occupation

Asthma that is present during the week but clears at weekends or on holiday. Sometimes there will be a very obvious relation to some particular process, such as soldering, colour printing, or preparing chemicals. Sometimes the symptoms will initially be running of the nose, or watering of the eyes, and only later will there be coughing and wheezing.

Certain sorts of occupational asthma develop more readily in atopic than in non-atopic subjects. The allergens which are involved tend to be the products of living things whether animal or plant. The asthma experienced by coffeepickers provides an example. On breathing in the aromatic vapour from raw coffee beans, they develop wheezing and running of the eyes and nose. Roasting the beans or boiling the coffee for three minutes destroys the allergen. This is a true atopic asthma. Yet many subjects developing occupational asthma have no previous history of allergy and are not atopic. This is the case with most of the workers developing asthma from inorganic materials though there is no sharply defined parallel between atopic/non-atopic and organic/inorganic.

The circumstances of exposure to the sensitizing agent are important. Length of time in the industry is a very crude index. Even with a single agent this timing is exceedingly variable. In the platinum industry, some workers develop wheezing within four months—others not for ten years. The degree of exposure—concentration of dust or vapour—whether it is intermittent or continuous—whether there is sufficient ventilation—where the workers stand or sit in the factory—all these and many other external factors influence whether or not asthma will develop.

Sometimes, once sensitization has occurred, tiny amounts of the same chemical will excite a reaction outside the working environment. A man employed in making the antibody Spiramycin became sensitized. He left the factory, but continued to wheeze. His wife, still employed in the same factory, was bringing enough antibiotic home in the dust on her clothes to cause her husband to wheeze. She left the factory. But still his wheeze did not entirely clear. The provoking agent was tracked down to eggs. Spiramycin is used to treat infection in battery hens. The minute amount of antibiotic which had found its way into the eggs was sufficient to trigger off his asthma.

Occupational asthmas can arise from environmental pollution. One factory recognizing that its processes were generating chemicals likely to cause asthma, fitted a ventilation system. The dust from this poured through the windows of the next door factory and the workers there developed asthma. Similarly residents in streets downwind from a

Occupation	Agents implicated
Animal handlers	Hair, dander, mites, insects.
Bakers	Flour dust, moulds, weevils
Chemical workers	Formalin, piperazine; sulphonamides, penicillin and other antibiotics; Isocyanates; Phthalic anhydride and epoxy resins
Coffee industry	Green coffee dust
Cotton workers	Cotton, flax, hemp
Detergent industry	Proteolytic enzymes
Domestics etc.	House dust
Electricians	Soldering fluxes
Meat packers	Fumes from polyvinyl film cut with hot wire
Metal workers	Nickel, vanadium, chromium
Oil extractors	Castor bean, linseed and cotton seed
Paint workers	Toluene diisocyanates
Photographic industry	Complex salts of platinum
Poultry workers	Feathers
Printers	Gum arabic, tragacanth
Rubber industry	Ethylene diamine and paraphenylene diamine
Wood workers	Dust from western red cedar, Iroko etc.

Fig. 22. A list of some of the commoner occupational asthmas.

92

Asthma and occupation

castor-oil extracting factory, found they were developing wheezy chests as a result of inhaling the smoke from the factory chimney.

There is now a huge list of industries in which some process or other has been implicated in the causation of occupational asthma. A list of some of the commoner ones is given. The interaction between the host— the asthmatic worker—and the sensitizing agent—dust, chemical, and so forth—is especially revealing in some examples and worth following through.

First and simplest, some subjects with previous or established atopic asthma, may find themselves encountering in their occupation allergens to which they are already sensitive. These will be simple environmental allergens to which any atopic asthmatic might react. Jockeys, shepherds, vets, and laboratory workers will handle horses, sheep, cats, rats, and other animals and may show asthmatic reactions to hair or skin dander. Domestics and factory cleaners will raise dusts containing the ubiquitous 'house' dust mite. In the cheese industry, in flour mills and granaries, moulds in the air can generate late asthmatic reactions.

The work of bakers illustrates how complex allergic asthma can be in the occupational setting, even when none other than naturally-occurring allergens have to be considered. As always Ramazzini has some pertinent observations to make: 'All kinds of grain . . . have mixed in with them a very fine dust . . . hence when it is necessary to sift wheat and barley . . . the men . . . are so plagued . . . that when the work is finished they heap a thousand curses on their calling.'

To many with established asthma the fine dust of flour is a simple irritant capable of setting up reflex bronchospasm. The flour can act as an allergen too. Atopic sensitivity to flour, demonstrable by positive prick tests and immediate onset bronchial challenges, is frequent. But in the flour and grain are unwanted visitors. Moulds such as *Aspergillus* and *Penicillium*, if the grain has been left to stand, and the grain weevil *Sitophilus granularis*.

Within a given bakery some of those with asthmatic symptoms will be sensitive to flour, some to moulds, some to weevils. In small bakeries over 40 per cent of the workers may develop asthma due to one or other of these agents. In larger bakeries, probably because of better ventilation and less direct handling of raw materials, the incidence may be only 10–20 per cent. Nonetheless even this is considerably more than that in the general population. Why? It seems chiefly because of the intensity of the exposure to otherwise common antigens.

Occupational asthmas in other settings occur through quite a different mechanism, namely exposure to relatively small concentrations of unusual and potentially highly-sensitizing substances not encountered outside industry. Locust handlers stand a very high chance of developing asthma. Here the allergen is highly potent but from a natural source. Three other examples of highly sensitizing agents illustrate further features of occupational asthma—the enzyme detergents, the complex salts of platinum, and the isocyanates.

Enzyme detergents

The enzyme detergents introduced into washing powders in the 1960s were a hazard not only to those involved in their manufacture but to the housewife as well. Sensitization was first evident in the skin with wealing and blistering. Then respiratory symptoms began to be recorded—stuffiness of the nose, sneezing, breathlessness, coughing, and chest pains. Challenge tests were devised mimicking occupational exposure. In an 'environmental' chamber—a relatively small enclosed space,—the suspect subjects tipped detergent from one container to another creating a dust of the detergent in the enclosed atmosphere. Spirometric tests revealed the development of asthmatic airflow obstruction. In some the reaction was immediate, in others late—in a few both immediate and late reactions appeared. So, all the types of allergic response described earlier were demonstrable. This particular observation is of great significance. Outside the occupational setting, at this time, aspergillus sensitivity had been the only one to show the complete range of allergic reactions. So it could have been a property peculiar to aspergillus. But here was another allergen showing the same phenomena. And with other occupational asthmas showing a similar pattern, it became obvious that the type of reaction produced was a property not of the allergen but of the host.

Two other important observations can be gleaned from the study of enzyme detergent asthma. First the demonstration of a specific immunological response in affected workers. The allergen turned out to be a derivative of the bacterium *Bacillus subtilis* used to create the enzyme for the detergent. Specific IgE antibodies were demonstrated in those workers giving immediate reactions on challenge testing, and specific precipitating IgG antibodies in those giving late reactions. So, immunologically this occupational asthma is pretty clearly and cleverly worked out.

The second message goes to the heart of occupational medicine: prevention. As soon as the risks were recognized, control measures were introduced; protective clothing, masks for the workers, and strict precautions in handling the raw detergent. The concentrate is now contained in impervious paper sacks or metal bins, and where possible handled by automatic machinery. Rooms where powder is released into the atmosphere are efficiently ventilated and regularly hosed down.

Platinum salts

The precious silvery-white metal platinum, discovered and named by the Spaniards in Colombia about 1735, is harmless in its pure metallic form. When used in industry in the form of complex chloride salts, it produces asthma in 100 per cent of workers exposed for five years or more. Those involved in extracting the metal and preparing its salts are most at risk. Dusts or sprays of a complex chemical called hexachloroplatinate are also found in the atmosphere in electroplating workshops, in photographic studio using plate toning, or in jewellers where the metal might be dissolved in aqua regia and treated with ammonium chloride. The first report came from Chicago in 1911. Eight workers in a photographic studio reported irritation of the throat and nose, sneezing and coughing. In England more than half of the workers in a precious metal refinery complained of similar symptoms together with more obvious asthmatic features—shortness of breath and wheezing. Neither the pure metal nor the salts of similar metals such as palladium caused any symptoms. It was only the compounds derived from platinum.

An allergic basis for platinum asthma is strongly suggested by the pattern of challenge tests—both immediate, late, and double reactions are again recorded. Skin prick tests too are positive to the hexochloroplatinate salts. The demonstration of antibodies in the blood has so far eluded research workers—but this does not seriously detract from the proposal that this too is an allergic asthma.

Isocyanates

Perhaps the situation with isocyanates is a little less clearcut. The main use of organic di-isocyanates is in the manufacture of polyurethane foams, though they are also used widely for making adhesives, synthetic rubbers, and paints. The highly reactive isocyanate molecules are allowed to react with resins under controlled conditions. Carbon dioxide, so evolved, bubbles up in the polyurethane to give a foam. Toluene di-isocyanate (TDI) is the compound most often used. It is highly volatile and a potent trigger for respiratory symptoms. Di-isocyanato-diohenle methane (MDI) produces a more rigid foam, is less volatile, and less of a hazard.

95

Asthma and occupation

The fumes of TDI are undoubtedly directly irritant to the nose, throat, and chest. Accidental exposure to toxic levels causes immediate breathlessness, coughing, sweating, and prostration which has led to death. Lower concentrations released during normal manufacturing processes give an irritating cough and asthmatic wheezing. On leaving the industry, sufferers mostly recover very quickly. However, in a few, subsequent exposure to very small concentrations of TDI has again caused asthmatic wheezing. This observation suggests allergy: but proof has been difficult to come by. Challenge tests have been devised. Using simulated natural exposure in environmental chambers, immediate, late, and double reactions have been recorded. Skin prick tests with TDI or with TDI joined to a human protein, do become positive in a proportion of workers exposed to TDI but the workers with positive tests do not necessarily develop sensitivity as judged by challenge testing, nor do those with positive challenge tests all have positive skin tests. The same discrepancy arises with other tests for immunological responses such as those looking for antibodies in the blood. So, occupational asthma to TDI is certainly an irritant phenomenon but whether it is also an allergic phenomenon is not yet quite certain.

With TDI it is worth remembering that exposure can occur outside the actual manufacturing industry. In the USA polyurethane foam 'do it yourself' kits have been marketed. They mimic the industrial process, and have two pressurized cans connected by tubing. The foam is produced when the contents of the two cans are mixed. Samples of the atmosphere around these cans when the reaction is created, have shown concentrations of TDI far above those that would be acceptable in industry. Chest symptoms have certainly been recorded in the home using these kits. Much more subtle is the exposure of previously sensitized subjects to small concentrations of TDI, when polyurethane foam is cut or crushed in the hand. One unexpected hazard occurred on the beaches of Cornwall when several drums of TDI were washed up on the shore and broke open releasing their toxic fumes.

Cotton

The oldest recognized occupational asthma is that which affects workers in the cotton and allied industries. It was recorded in Lancashire in 1831 by Kay though not described in detail till thirty or forty years later when it was named byssinosis. The name comes from the Greek word for fine linen or flax. Inevitably Ramazzini had watched the dressers of flax and hemp, and the carders of silk rolls and described

Asthma and occupation

their ailments: 'Now the men who comb these rolls are attacked by a terrible cough and serious difficulty in respiration.' The combing of cotton fibres into parallel strands was once carried out with thistle heads (hence the term carding from the Latin word for a thistle). Even done by hand it was a dusty occupation. When the great and clumsy machines of the industrial revolution swung into action, the air was filled with cotton dust. Some dust was created in the mixing room where the cotton bales were opened, and rather more in the blow room where the cotton was beaten and blown to eliminate contamination. But the strippers and grinders in charge of the carding engines were most at risk.

Byssinosis has features that set it apart from the other occupational asthmas. The most characteristic of these is Monday morning tightness. Schilling recorded it in these words of a Lancashire cotton stripper: 'Monday is a different day to me. Getting to 11o'clock I feel tight in the chest and short of wind . . . Towards 5.30 I feel done and struggle for breath . . . I am a dead horse on Mondays but could fell a bull on Tuesdays.' Up to a quarter of those working in the blow rooms and a third of those in the carding rooms might develop symptoms like this after about ten years in the mills. This Monday inconvenience becomes serious when symptoms persist through other days of the week. Recovery still occurs to some degree at weekends and especially on holiday. If the workers stay in the industry, a final stage of permanent disability follows. Now that this has been recognized it is not allowed to happen in the Lancashire cotton mills, but respiratory disability is still common in juteworkers and hemp workers in other parts of the world.

The Monday tightness is associated with changes in lung function tests that indicates that narrowing of the airways is responsible for the symptoms: but why the curious distribution in the week, why the chronic disease? Answers to these questions are not complete, but allergens here seem one of the least likely explanations. Blood tests do show some antibody formation to components of cotton dust but the presence of these seems to bear little relation to chest symptoms. This is an example where there does appear to be a direct chemical influence of the cotton dust on the airways. Laboratory experiments have shown that extracts of cotton dust can cause histamine to be released from the lungs: and histamine causes airways to narrow. Neat cotton dust will cause tightness not only in mill workers but also in normal subjects never previously exposed to cotton, if given in high enough concentration. Carefully washed cotton dust will not give this reaction: nor will it release histamine from lung tested in the laboratory. Why do the

97

Asthma and occupation

symptoms wane during the week? Presumably because stores of histamine become depleted. And why do symptoms return so vigorously after the weekend off? Presumably because stores are replenished. But this is almost certainly too simplistic. Histamine is but one of several substances released in the lung in atopic allergic asthma. Why it should behave differently in the cotton workers and why it should lead to chronic disabling disease is not known.

Whilst occupational asthmas hold much of interest for those involved with the management of this disorder, perhaps three points stand out beyond any others. The first concerns the nature of atopic allergy. It has long been thought that atopy is found in only a relatively small subsection of the population, about one in ten. This must now be qualified. Atopic sensitivity to commonly encountered environmental allergens is only found in this group. But it emerges from the study of occupational asthmas that heavy exposure to certain allergens—of which locusts and the complex salts of platinum seem to be good examples—can produce atopic sensitivity both in the skin and in the airways in much higher proportion of the exposed population.

Secondly the occupational asthmas confirm the impression given by some other allergic asthmas that a combination of immediate and late asthmatic reactions is quite common. This goes a long way towards reconciling the differences between naturally occurring asthma, in which attacks last many hours or even days—with challenge tests, which if confined to a consideration of immediate reactions are all over in a couple of hours.

Finally the potential for cure exists more realistically in relation to the occupational asthmas than it does in respect to any other form of asthma. Even for this reason alone they require the most careful analysis and investigation.

9

Asthma worldwide

CLUES to the causation of illness can often be picked up by taking a global rather than a parochial view. Malaria is only contracted in certain parts of the world. These parts are generally hot and humid. It turns out that climate influences malaria by providing appropriate breeding conditions for the Anopholes mosquito. Through the bite of this insect, malaria is passed on from one person to another. The analysis of such environmental conditions has contributed immeasurably to the discovery of the causes of many of the major epidemic illnesses of the world.

This approach, which began as a study of epidemics of infectious diseases, which from time to time sweep across the globe, has long since extended its horizons to look at non-infectious diseases. Epidemiology is concerned with the pattern of diseases on a larger scale than that observable in single patients. The pattern of diseases in families, in groups, and in races, is examined to determine the frequency with which the disorder is seen, the age range of afflicted persons and the personal, climatic, and environmental factors that seem to be associated with the disease under study. Epidemiological research can be applied to asthma. From this research some fascinating facts emerge, but before lining these up for appraisal, some cautionary notes must be sounded.

First, for sensible and reliable answers to any questions about asthma, the condition must be accurately defined. Regrettably this has not always been so in epidemiological studies of asthma. To be fair the difficulties are formidable. They centre around the dilemma of detail versus numbers. The stricter the criteria used to define asthma, the more elaborate needs to be the questioning and testing. This takes time and personnel, and means that limits are set on the number of subjects that can be assessed. On the other hand epidemiological research is best served by studying large numbers of subjects. Indeed best of all served by questioning everyone in a given community. The definition of asthma under these circumstances may have to rely on nothing more than the questions 'do you have asthma?' or 'do you have wheezing?' The answer to the first of these questions will depend not only on what the person being questioned believes about asthma, but also on what their doctor considers is asthma, and how much he has communicated his opinion to his patient. Wheezing, although an important audible accompaniment of asthma, occurs as noted earlier in other conditions and so is even less reliable in guiding epidemiological research than is a question about asthma itself.

If the first danger concerns the definition of asthma, the second concerns timing. Asthma, by its nature, is an intermittent disorder. So the question 'do you have asthma?' must be qualified. 'Do you have asthma today?' or 'Have you had asthma at any time in your life?' The answers to these questions give two figures for the frequency of asthma. Both are termed a prevalence. The first will be a point prevalence referring to all cases of asthma identified as present on the day the study is carried out. The second is a cumulative prevalence and includes in addition, those subjects who might have seasonal asthma or who were asthmatic as children. Intermediate between these two is a period prevalence in which all subjects having asthma within a specified period are recorded.

The third danger in looking for epidemiological clues is more subtle. It concerns what other information should be gathered beyond the answers to the questions giving a prevalence figure. These questions depend on the preconceptions of the investigator. So the emphasis placed and the details recorded of climate, of industrialization, of race, of social class and custom, of environmental allergens, and so forth, will vary from survey to survey. The extent to which this information is recorded will colour and determine the conclusions that can be drawn from the study.

With these reservations in mind, what are the epidemiological facts about asthma and how can they be interpreted?

Asthma is not equally common in all parts of the world. In the highlands of Papua New Guinea asthma is so rare that the local population have no word for it. On Tristan da Cunha almost half the islanders give a history of asthma. Between these extremes, figures for the UK and USA show asthma to occur at some stage in 2–4 per cent of children and 4–6 per cent of adults.

Setting aside the question of the definition of asthma and the type of prevalence recorded, the influences that can give rise to variations on a scale such as this are various, but they can be grouped together under two broad headings: nature and nurture. Nature is the inherited genetic make-up, which in its broadest sense means racial origin, and which, for the individual, means the family characteristics handed on from parents to children. Nurture implies environmental influence whether this be the effects of cultural habits and life style, or external factors such as climate or exposure to allergens.

100

Asthma worldwide

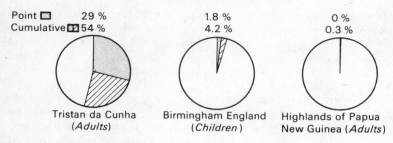

Point ▨	29 %	1.8 %	0 %
Cumulative ▨	54 %	4.2 %	0.3 %

Tristan da Cunha
(*Adults*)

Birmingham England
(*Children*)

Highlands of Papua
New Guinea (*Adults*)

Fig. 23. Point and cumulative prevalences for asthma in three localities.

The populations which appear at the two extremes of the prevalence list are both highly inbred. Of the fifteen original settlers on the remote south Atlantic island of Tristan da Cunha, three had asthma. All three were women, two from St Helena and one from England. The volcano on Tristan da Cunha erupted in 1961 and the islanders were temporarily resettled in Britain. Medical checks emphasized the very high prevalence of asthma. The point prevalence—the number of cases actually wheezing on the day they were examined—was as high as 29 per cent for the adults and 12 per cent for the children. The change in environment to this country brought the islanders no relief from their persistent asthma. Investigations for allergy revealed no provoking agent present on Tristan da Cunha that could not be found elsewhere: indeed the commonest allergen was the ubiquitous house dust mite. Infection did commonly trigger their asthma but their minimal contact with the rest of the world meant that epidemics of infection occurred sporadically brought in by visitors from passing ships. Psychological stress was not a feature of island life. So there is no escape from the conclusion that the islanders had inherited a tendency to asthma from their forbears which had been intensified by inbreeding.

How important genetic factors are in determining differences between other races is less easy to discover. Papua New Guinea where asthma is very uncommon is a relatively short distance to the north of Australia where as many as one in twenty of the adult population have asthma. There are obvious differences on several counts between Australia and Papua New Guinea, despite their relative proximity. The Papua New Guinea figures refer to the indigenous tribal population. This is an inbred group of primitive people whose racial and cultural characteristics obviously differ drastically from the white population from whom the Australian prevalence figures were taken. Reliable figures do not

101

Asthma worldwide

seem to be available to compare Australian aboriginals with the Papua New Guinea natives, but there are other primitive peoples who have similarly low figures: American Indians and the Eskimos. In Northern Canada only three Eskimos were admitted to hospital for asthma over as long as twelve years. The estimated prevalence rate was 0.08 per cent—one in 1200.

The natives of Papua New Guinea and the Eskimos are unlikely to have much genetic material in common. They certainly do not share similar climatic conditions. But some parallels can be drawn between the life styles of these two communities. Perhaps the greatest amongst these might be their basically rural economy and lack of industrialization. An influence due to urbanization seems to play a part in the prevalence of asthma in the west African state of Gambia. Asthma is virtually unknown amongst villagers from rural communities. Just one case was on the files in a community of 1200. Yet in a town only 100 miles away, the hospital treated eight cases of asthma each day. Likewise in urban populations from Kenya, Ghana, Zambia, and Nigeria asthma would appear to be a common problem. No breakdown of prevalence between urban and rural communities in western countries suggest anything like the striking differences recorded in less-developed parts of the world.

The movement of people from a place with a low prevalence of asthma into urban communities offers interesting but not totally concordant information. Australasia provides another example. When the Tokelau Islands in the southern Pacific were hit by a hurricane, facilities were made available for the setting up of a Tokelau community in Wellington, New Zealand. The migrants began to complain increasingly of asthma. A careful survey showed that the Tokelau children living in New Zealand had twice as much asthma as those who had remained in their native islands, and very much more eczema.

Birmingham schoolchildren of all races have been carefully surveyed for asthma by Dr Morrison-Smith. Negro children born in the West Indies have a lower prevalence of asthma than caucasian children born in the United Kingdom. But West Indian children born in the UK have a similar prevalence to UK caucasian children. Is the influence urbanization or something else connected with western civilization? Asian children born in India also have a lower prevalence of asthma than UK caucasian children. But here the comparison fails. Asian children born in the UK do not show an increase in asthma as the West Indian children did or the Tokelau Islanders did. Could this be because Asian families are less closely integrated into the local urban communities?

Asthma worldwide

A pattern begins to emerge. There seems to be some factor in urbanization, that allows asthma to become more common. This prompts a search for factors in the urban environment that might be responsible.

Returning first to Africa, a chance observation provoked a search for some link between parasitic diseases and asthma. British naval officers stationed in the Gambia reported less hayfever at times when they developed parasitic infections. In rural Africans, worm infestation is common: in the towns it is less so. The implication was drawn that the urban population in ridding themselves of intestinal parasites, at the same time became more liable to asthma.

Worm infestations excite an antibody response which is of the IgE type. The antibodies are specific to the parasite, and appear in the serum in large quantities. Both in the Gambia and in Zaria the rural populations had a higher level of IgE than subjects from the towns. In the asthmatics there was a much lower level of IgE than in the non-asthmatics. IgE is an essential component in the allergic mechanisms for asthma. As described earlier it is the combination of IgE with allergen on the surface of the mast cell that causes the release from that cell of the chemical mediators that seem responsible for airways narrowing. The hypothesis proposed is that in the parasite-infested subjects, the mast cells become so saturated with IgE directed against the parasite that they do not have room for allergen IgE. So asthma cannot be induced.

Laboratory studies have lent some support to this idea. Lung tissue exposed to high concentration of parasite IgE will not readily accept allergen IgE. Dr Godfrey who carried out the Gambian study which supports this concept put it this way, 'The idea that allergic disorders may represent the continuing activity of an immune system made redundant by man's cleanliness, has attraction.' It does, but is it true?

Support for the observation that asthma is lower in rural than in urban African children has been given from surveys in South Africa and Rhodesia but not from Tanzania. In a rural Tanzanian community asthma was not uncommon. On the basis of exercise-induced wheezing, the point prevalence was 8 per cent. Furthermore there was no difference in the degree of parasitic infection or in the total serum IgE levels between those with and those without asthma, so that parasitic infestation did not appear to protect these children from developing asthma. This clearly casts some doubt on the hypothesis, though no direct comparison with urban children was made. If asthma is more common in the towns and the inverse relationship with worm infestation does not hold true, is there another possible explanation? One has been offered that is related to cultural habits.

103

Asthma worldwide

Movement of peoples from a rural to an urban way of life is often asosciated with a decrease in the extent to which children are breastfed. In the first six months of life the child's chief nourishment is from milk. If the mother's milk is replaced by cows' milk, the exposure of the infant to foreign and potentially allergenic protein material will be increased. It does appear that avoidance of cows' milk by atopic children greatly reduces their chances of developing eczema. Whether this is also true of asthma remains to be seen. In view of the close association between eczema and asthma in infants, it can be hoped that this will be so. Infant feeding habits point to this explanation in some of the communities mentioned. There is no doubt that all Papua New Guinea children are breastfed. On the other hand, though West Indian children born in Birmingham are breastfed twice as often as caucasian children, they develop positive skin tests for atopic allergy just as frequently. Breastfeeding may be an important means of protecting infants from developing asthma, but so far the evidence is not conclusive.

It is unlikely that any unifying hypothesis can explain all the differences in the prevalence of asthma in various communities. Some figures on the map (Fig. 24) highlight further anomalies. Amongst the Japanese, a highly industrialized and urbanized race, there appears to be a low prevalence of asthma in children, 0.7 per cent: even allowing for the fact that this is a point prevalence based on those children wheezing on the day of study, rather than a cumulative prevalence of all those children who had at any time had asthma, the figure is lower than in most western nations. In western European communities the races that provide yet further contradictory figures are the Scandinavians. Again the prevalence is apparently quite low, about 1 per cent, and lowest of all in the most northern people, the Finns. Yet in Scotland just across the North Sea, 4.8 per cent of Aberdeen schoolchildren were found to have had asthma within one year of being examined. Whether it is race, class, way of life, industry, urbanization, or some other imponderable that explains these differences is not known.

Social differences apart from the question of breastfeeding, have at times figured in the asthma story. It was at one time suggested that children from the upper social classes were more prone to asthma. This certainly seemed to be so in Denver, Colorado, and also when school doctors' records from the Isle of Wight were analysed. By contrast in Vancouver asthma did not vary in prevalence between the social classes, and amongst Aberdeen schoolchildren there was an excess of asthma in the children of semi-skilled and unskilled manual workers. A Swedish study which embraced all aspects of daily life also

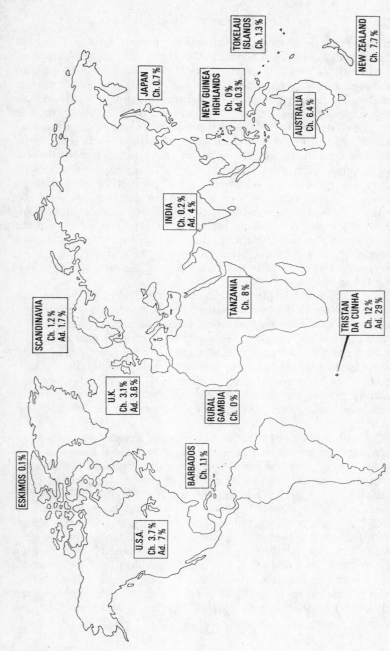

Fig. 24. Worldwide prevalence of asthma: an approximate view based on reported point and cumulative prevalence figures. Ch = children, Ad = adult.

ESKIMOS 0.1%

SCANDINAVIA
Ch. 1.2 %
Ad. 1.7 %

U.S.A.
Ch. 3.7%
Ad. 7 %

U.K.
Ch. 3.1%
Ad. 3.6%

BARBADOS
Ch. 1.1%

RURAL
GAMBIA
Ch. 0%

TRISTAN
DA CUNHA
Ch. 12%
Ad. 29%

TANZANIA
Ch. 8 %

INDIA
Ch. 0.2%
Ad. 4 %

JAPAN
Ch. 0.7 %

NEW GUINEA
HIGHLANDS
Ch. 0%
Ad. 0.3%

TOKELAU
ISLANDS
Ch. 1.3 %

AUSTRALIA
Ch. 6.4%

NEW ZEALAND
Ch. 7.7 %

Asthma worldwide

concluded that neither social class nor family income directly influenced asthma. It did however pick out lack of central heating or a bathroom as signifcant factors. This is worth tying in with observations made in London and Leiden in Holland. In these cities asthmatics were often found to live in old houses built on badly drained soil and close to canals or underground streams. Dampness and poor heating are just the conditions favoured by the house dust mite and many of the asthmatics were dust sensitive. Thus a chain of circumstances leads from social class to living conditions through to exposure to a common allergen.

It is often difficult to decide whether the environment influences asthma by encouraging an allergen or whether it operates through climatic changes. Many patients would argue the importance of the weather in triggering asthmatic attacks. Damp and cold feature prominently. Coastland dwellers in South Africa gained relief by moving inland where it was warmer and drier. Similar observations have been made in Spain, Israel, and Brazil. A drop in air temperature will act non-specifically as a bronchial irritant in asthmatics and in many chronic bronchitics.

In a casualty department in Brisbane, careful records showed that emergency attendances by asthmatics at night varied with temperature and humidity. A sharp drop in atmospheric temperature, often with the formation of mist or fog, seemed to set off a spate of asthma attacks. But here, and elsewhere, there was also a more general increase in asthma associated with the damp autumnal and winter months. Perhaps the cold weather drives the asthmatic indoors where he is more continuously exposed to house dust allergens. Perhaps it is the occurrence of viral chest infections, encouraged by the weather conditions, that is important.

The way in which environmental and other factors operate together to produce an unusual pattern is illustrated by what is known as New Orleans asthma. This town has experienced some remarkable outbreaks of asthma, clustered in the autumn months. For example 350 cases of asthma were admitted to one 3200 bed hospital in a single 24-hour period on October 26 1955. These were attacks of genuine asthma mostly in previously known atopic asthmatics with characteristics not differing from those seen at other seasons. The autumn in New Orleans is a time of adverse climatic change. Meteorological analysis suggested that low wind speed, low relative humidity, and low temperature at night all combined to allow a build-up of naturally-occurring allergens such as mould spores. But why the sudden rush of cases over such a short period? A more careful look at the community showed that in many of the admitted cases, the asthma had been building up over some weeks. The community is one of low income and medical attention outside the hospital is expensive and scarce. It seemed that most of these asthmatics were forced to accept increasing wheeziness and only cried for help when it became intolerable. When one did so, something of a chain reaction was set up in the neighbourhood, so that a large number of patients presented to the hospital services in a very short time.

The atmosphere is not just a vehicle for climatic change. Air pollution of local importance in occupational asthma, is of general importance and concern when it contaminates the enviroment of whole cities. Sulphur dioxide is the chief culprit. Given off in excessively high concentrations in volcanic eruptions it probably caused the death of Pliny the elder. His nephew recorded during the Vesuvius eruption of A.D. 79 that 'as he slept his breathing was rather loud and heavy'. The following morning . . . 'he stood leaning on two slaves and then suddenly collapsed, I imagine because the dense fumes choked his breathing by blocking his windpipe which was constitutionally weak and narrow and often inflamed.'

Sulphur dioxide is a powerful irritant to the bronchial tree. The airways tighten within ten seconds of inhaling it. Respiratory disease in a community can be correlated with the amount of sulphur dioxide in the atmosphere: asthmatics have more attacks: bronchitics wheeze more readily. Heavy industrial pollution was probably responsible for the high incidence of asthma in US military personnel in the Tokyo-Yokohama region of Japan. These men suffered recurrent wheezing attacks in the autumn and early winter months which cleared when they returned to the USA. Though most were heavy smokers, they also showed atopic features such as positive skin tests. It seems likely that the acrid fumes from industrial pollution were creating asthma in susceptible individuals.

This bird's eye view of the geography of asthma has served to emphasize again the dual influences of external and inherited forces. Climatic and socioeconomic circumstances cannot alone induce asthma to those not so inherently predisposed. Equally, given an inherited tendency to asthma, the environment—whether this be in terms of exposure to allergens, adverse weather conditions, industrialization, or domestic circumstances—can play a role in either facilitating or suppressing the expression of asthma. Thus whether viewed in the individual or in whole communities, there is no escape from the conclusion that asthma is truly a multifactorial disorder. It is the summation of the effects of inheritance and environment that determines whether asthma will or will not be experienced. The addition of one further trigger factor, however minor it might be on its own, may be sufficient to bring the underlying tendency to asthma out in the open. Conversely what might be of itself a minor adjustment in environment or medical management, may be all that is required to convert a troublesome persistent asthma to a mild and occasional wheezing. So we turn in the next few chapters to the question of the treatment of asthma.

10

Bronchodilators

THE large measure of success currently achieved in the control of the symptoms of asthma centres on the use of one particular class of remedy, the bronchodilators. These are medicines which 'open up' the narrowed airways by an action primarily on bronchial muscle.

In the description of the autonomic nervous system in Chapter 3, a distinction was drawn between its sympathetic and parasympathetic divisions. It is the former that prepares the animal for activity, whilst the latter deals with more restful functions. As far as the lungs are con- centred, the parasympathetic nervous system is well represented in the vagus nerve. This, it will be recalled, is responsible for various reflexes including the bronchial narrowing which occurs in response to the in- halation of irritants. Sympathetic nerves on the other hand do not seem to figure at all in the nerve supply of the bronchial muscle. At first sight this might seem a distinct disadvantage since sympathetic activity is associated with relaxation of bronchial muscle, just the result wanted in treating asthma. Fortunately the muscle is responsive to the chemical messengers, or neurotransmitters, of the autonomic nervous system, whether or not it is supplied by specific autonomic nerves. Indeed the body depends on this fact for a rapid mobilization of sympathetic activity in emergency situations.

This was discovered under unusual circumstances by a general prac- titioner Dr Oliver towards the end of the last century. He became interested in extracts obtained from various animal glands. His experi- ments were performed by injecting the extracts under the skin of members of his own family. With calf adrenal gland extract he noted a narrowing of the radial artery and concluded that there must have been a rise in blood pressure. Oliver took his ideas to a sceptical Pro- fessor Schafer, who in the words of Sir Henry Dale, found himself standing 'like some watcher of the skies when a new planet swims into his ken' watching the mercury rise in the manometer with amazing

Bronchodilators

rapidity and to an astounding height. Dale was involved with the purification of adrenal gland extracts, eventually isolating adrenaline and noradrenaline. Studies over subsequent years revealed that in states of acute stress the adrenal medulla secretes its hormones into the bloodstream to mobilize sympathetic activity rapidly. Adrenaline proved to be the main hormone in the adrenal gland together with small amounts of noradrenaline, whereas the sympathetic nerve endings contained noradrenaline alone.

When administered to man, both adrenaline and noradrenaline circulate throughout the body causing changes which are similar to those caused by the activation of the nerves of the sympathetic nervous system. It was very soon discovered that as far as the chest was concerned, adrenaline would open up the bronchi, but noradrenaline would not. The commercial development of adrenaline as a bronchodilator for asthma followed in the 1920s.

This was not by any means the beginning of bronchodilator therapy. A 4000-year-old Chinese herbal remedy, Ma Huang, a cough linctus, contained the first known bronchodilator, ephedrine. In Roman times Pliny the elder recorded that ephedrine was taken in sweet wine, for the treatment of asthma. Thereafter it seems forgotten till this century. In 1913 Japanese investigators isolated ephedrine and it was marketed there as 'Asthmatol'. Ephedrine was the first class of drug which possessed properties which mimic the action of the sympathetic nerves and so are called sympathomimetic.

So, some fifty years ago physicians were in a position to prescribe two powerful bronchodilator drugs; adrenaline and ephedrine. Adrenaline was prepared as a solution for injecting and for inhalation. Ephedrine was prepared as a tablet. Adrenaline was the standby treatment for acute asthma for doctors and patients over many years. Injected subcutaneously, slowly, in small quantities it was a powerful remedy.

There followed attempts to manufacture in the laboratory compounds with similar properties to these naturally-occurring substances. Of the many such compounds one stood out as highly effective—this was isoprenaline. As an aerosol for inhalation, it established itself as a potent and very rapidly acting bronchodilator.

But adrenaline, ephedrine, and isoprenaline all have their problems. They are not only relaxants of bronchial smooth muscle but also general stimulants of all parts of the sympathetic nervous system. This means that the blood pressure rises, the pulse races, the head thumps, and the pupils constrict. Ephedrine also affects the bladder, and causes

Bronchodilators

anxiety and excitement. If the adrenaline is injected into a vein rather than being absorbed from under the skin, the action on the heart can be dangerous. Thus a search went on for more selective agents.

Some hope was engendered into this research when it was discovered that not all the sympathetic nerve-muscle junctions behaved in the same way. Ahlquist postulated that there were two types; alpha and beta. Furthermore he affirmed the notion that all the involuntary muscles of the body were capable of responding to circulating adrenaline and noradrenaline whether or not they were supplied by sympathetic nerves. However, not every muscle had the same receptors. In the bronchial muscle the beta receptors seemed to predominate: there were alpha receptors on blood vessels which when stimulated caused the vessels to constrict. Beta receptors were also present in the heart.

Perhaps of even greater clinical value than the division of receptors into alpha and beta divisions was the recognition that not all beta receptors were identical. Those in the heart were labelled, beta 1, those in the bronchi, beta 2. The great importance of this discovery lay, of course, in the potential for finding drugs that would relax beta 2 receptors—and so relieve asthma—without having a stimulant action on the heart through the beta 1 receptors. The work to achieve this end has been one of the most important contributions of the pharmaceutical industry to asthma over the last fifteen years.

A daunting array of bronchodilators has been produced. Apart from introducing selectivity of action on beta 2 receptors, it has been the aim of the pharmaceutical chemists to prolong the duration of the effect of these drugs without losing the immediacy of relief that is so much coveted by the patient. A list of the sympathomimetic broncho-dilators currently available is given in the table (Fig. 25). Salbutamol remains the most frequently prescribed longer acting beta 2 selective bronchodilator. Orciprenaline, used less now than previously, was less selective than more recently synthesized drugs. Terbutaline is very similar to salbutamol, and is used extensively in Scandinavia. Like fenoterol it has a somewhat longer duration of action than salbutamol. Rimiterol, on the other hand, acts for a rather shorter time.

Duration of action is most certainly a property that can be built into a sympathomimetic bronchodilator. Speed of onset of action is very similar for all of them, though after the initial boost there may be a slow build-up of effect for about an hour with longer-acting drugs. It is not very meaningful to talk about the relative potency of these various drugs. The degree of relief possible depends on many factors of which only a few are directly related to the drug itself. Any of the

111

UK approved name	Tablets	Aerosols	Injection	UK trade names	Other approved names	Other trade names
ADRENALINE			✓		EPINEPHRINE (US) EPINEPHRINUM (IP)	Mistura (US) Epifrin (Aus)
EPHEDRINE	✓	✓		Medihaler -Epi	EPHENDRIUM (IP)	Ectasule Minus (US)
FENOTEROL		✓		Berotec		
ISOETHARINE	✓			Numotac		
ISOPRENALINE	✓	✓		Aleudrin, Medihaler-Iso	ISOPROTERENOL (US)	Isuprel (Aus) Proternol (US)
ORCIPRENALINE	✓	✓		Alupent	METAPROTERENOL (US)	Metaprel (US)
RIMITEROL		✓		Pulmadil		
SALBUTAMOL	✓	✓	✓	Ventolin	ALBUTEROL	
TERBUTALINE	✓	✓	✓	Bricanyl, Filair		Brethine (US) Feevone (Aus)

IP = International Pharmacopoeia   US = United States of America   Aus = Australia

Fig. 25. A list of sympathomimetic bronchodilators in common use.

Bronchodilators

sympathomimetic bronchodilators can be given in a dose that will produce the maximum effect possible in a given subject at a given time. The most potent reason for not giving a drug in maximum dose would be an unwanted side effect. With a non-selective drug such as iso-prenaline the side effect limiting its use would probably be a fast pulse rate or a rise in blood pressure. With the more selective agents, cardiac effects are much less but there can arise a distressing tremor especially of the hands.

Setting aside the inbuilt properties of the drug itself, the most important determinants of the degree of response expected from a bronchodilator lie with the individual. Some types of asthma, or some stages of asthma in an individual, are more reversible than others. The efficacy of a bronchodilator will depend to what degree actual bronchial muscle contraction is responsible for the airways' narrowing. Sympathomimetic agents cannot decrease mucus, though by relaxing the airways and stimulating the action of the cilia they do help it to come up. Then there is the question of the initial level of airways' narrowing. In general, in the severely obstructed asthmatic, a broncho-dilator will seem to have little effect. Likewise if there is minimal obstruction, the potential for improvement is small and again there will appear to be little benefit gained. It is in the very broad range of intermediate degrees of obstruction from mild to moderately severe that bronchodilators are most effective.

Lastly, in looking at how effective the bronchodilator is, we must discuss the question of route of administration. All bronchodilators are most effective dose for dose when injected. This is neither desirable nor practical for the everyday management of asthma. It is important for the treatment of acute asthma in hospital or by the general practitioner at home, and that aspect will be considered later. Facilities for patients to inject themselves with adrenaline are rarely provided now, both because of the ease with which other routes can give relief and because of the potential danger of the adrenaline. So that for general use there are but two routes to consider—by mouth or by inhalation.

Since most medicines are taken by mouth there is a time-honoured custom in favour of this route. All but the sickest patient can swallow. If a tablet or capsule is unpalatable, there are mixtures or syrups available. Not all can use an inhaler. Perhaps the old-fashioned bulb atomizers were the easiest. The bronchodilator was dissolved in water and a rubber bulb pumped to create a fine spray. Co-ordination with breathing, though it helped the economical use of the drug, was not essential. But this type of inhaler is rarely seen now. All the currently available

113

Bronchodilators

sympathomimetic bronchodilators are prepared in pressurised inhalers. The drug is dissolved in a mixture of organic solvents and locked under pressure in a small cannister. A jet of drug of measured size is released by pressing the cannister into its plastic casing. To inhale the drug the cannister must be triggered just as a breath in is being taken following a full breath out. Some find this difficult. The very young, the elderly, the handicapped, or the just plain ham-fisted seem unable to coordinate the breath in with the triggering of the inhaler. So for these the tablets might be preferable.

Two tricks to overcome this problem and still retain the inhaled route have been tried. A device known as the autohaler, in which a breath in triggered an internal mechanism for depressing the cannister, failed largely because the noise produced created a reflex closing of the throat, stopping the drug from being inhaled. The more recently introduced Rotahaler looks as though it may be more successful. The bronchodilator is in powder form and contained in a capsule. It is put inside the rotahaler which has the means for slicing the capsule and so releasing the powder. The powder is then inhaled as a cloud by the action of breathing in from the device. The principle, though not the design details, is similar to that for the spinhaler for sodium cromoglycate, which will be mentioned in Chapter 12.

Despite these problems with inhalers, there remains one powerful and overriding argument in their favour. Inhalers deliver a small dose of a potent bronchodilator directly to the organ in trouble, the lungs. Tablets or syrups taken by mouth must rely on much larger quantities of the drug being absorbed from the stomach and intestines in order to make available an adequate quantity for the lungs. Thus for salbutamol one inhalation contains 100 micrograms of the drug: one tablet contains two milligrams—twenty times the dose of the inhalation. Thus the potential for side effects will be many times greater than when using inhaler therapy. This fact is not significantly offset by the observation that there is a strong tendency for patients to take more puffs from their inhaler than recommended either by doctors or the pharmaceutical companies. This is in striking contrast to the general attitude towards tablets. It is usual that fewer tablets are taken than the number recommended and almost never more.

This being so, how and when should inhalers be used? There are basically three patterns of use for bronchodilator aerosols: for symptoms as they arise, as a preventative, anticipating symptoms, and regular use. Bronchodilators were originally seen as a means of giving symptomatic relief for episodic wheezing. They are still employed by many patients

114

Bronchodilators

(1) Remove the cover from the mouthpiece. Hold the inhaler as illustrated and shake vigorously.

(2) Breathe out slowly but no further than the end of a natural breath and then IMMEDIATELY ...

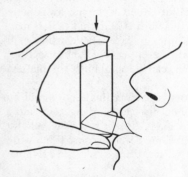

(3) Place the mouthpiece above the tongue and well into the mouth. Close the lips tightly round the mouthpiece. Press the top of the canister down firmly between forefinger and thumb whilst inhaling deeply and quickly.

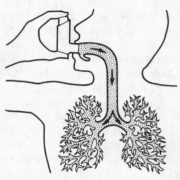

(4) Continue inhaling to carry the spray deep into the lungs. Hold the breath for as long as it is comfortable. Release pressure on the canister, remove the inhaler from your mouth, and breathe out *gently*.

Fig. 26. How to use an inhaler.

solely for this purpose. The chest becomes tight during the night, a wheeze develops walking up a hill. A puff from a bronchodilator aerosol will bring instant relief. For patients with mild asthma that for the most part is causing them no symptoms, and for patients with more severe asthma maintained on other therapy but having intermittent and unexpected spasms of wheezing, the inhaler is the friend they need.

With years of experience the pattern of use of bronchodilator

115

Bronchodilators

aerosols worked out by patients and doctors has changed. Specific types of preventative measure are to be discussed in Chapter 12. But there are circumstances where the bronchodilator aerosol can be used as a preventative. The wheezing that is seen after exercise can be prevented in almost all subjects by the prior inhalation of a bronchodilator aerosol. Other potentially wheeze-provoking situations can also be anticipated. An asthmatic sensitive to dogs could well take a puff from a bronchodilator aerosol before an unavoidable visit to a dog-keeping household.

When wheezing occurs frequently during the day or night, whether it follows a fixed pattern or occurs haphazardly, then regular aerosol bronchodilator therapy has much to offer. With a duration of action of 5–6 hours it is possible by taking a regular two puffs, three or four times daily to maintain a useful level of bronchodilation throughout the waking hours, and often through the night. Covering the small hours of the morning and especially the low point about dawn and awakening time, is not always feasible with the inhaler. It is here that tablets may come into their own. A form of salbutamol is available which will slowly release the active bronchodilator over a 10–12 hour period. Taken before going to bed at night this can often abolish the distress occasioned by the morning 'dip'.

I wonder how many asthmatic patients reading this section will be saying 'but my doctor tells me that inhalers can be dangerous and I should use them sparingly'? I hope not many. But it is a view held by some and one that must be discussed in some detail because it has wide implications. The view arose out of what has been called the epidemic of asthma deaths in the 1960s.

The story begins in 1961 though it was not noticed for a further three years. Deaths from asthma had been running along at a very low level for nearly 100 years since records were first made. The rate varied with age. For the five to thirty-four years age group one in every 100 deaths could be attributed to asthma. By 1966 the figure has risen to 3.4 per cent. In the ten to fourteen years age group the change was even more striking, a sevenfold increase, making asthma the fourth commonest cause of death at this age. Examination of case histories showed that a high proportion of the deaths were unanticipated and three quarters occurred outside hospitals.

An intensive search went on for a cause. There emerged what appeared to be a convincing argument, implicating pressurized aerosols. It was during the 1960s that these agents were becoming increasingly popular. Recorded prescription sales soared during these years reaching

Bronchodilators

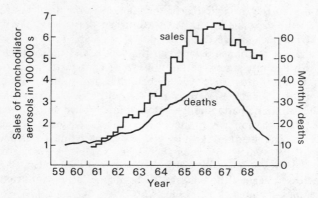

Fig. 27. Sales of bronchodilator aerosols and deaths from asthma in the 5–34 years age group during the 1960s. (Based on data from Drs W. H. W. Inman and A. M. Adelskein, *Lancet*, 1969)

a peak in 1966-7. In addition up to 1968 these agents could be bought 'over the counter' in chemists. Drs Inman and Adelstein pointed out the very suggestive parallel between the increase in asthma deaths and the increase in sales of bronchodilator aerosols (Fig. 27). Some 11 million aerosols were sold in England and Wales between 1961 and 1967 and 87 per cent of these contained isoprenaline rather than the selective beta 2 sympathomimetic drugs which were only just being introduced. It was supposed that the drugs had been taken in excessive dose and that the stimulant action of isoprenaline on the heart was responsible for the deaths. The argument gained strength when following advice from the Committee for the Safety of Medicines, prescriptions for aerosols containing a high concentration of isoprenaline fell. So did asthma deaths.

But the hypothesis was not perfect. The passage of time and the accumulation of other evidence has now cast considerable doubt on the proposal that the bronchodilator aerosols were responsible for the epidemic. This new evidence runs like this. First the epidemic was not evident in all countries. There was a rise in deaths in New Zealand and Australia as in the United Kingdom. But in Australia the rise in aerosol sales followed rather than preceeded the rise in asthma deaths. In Sweden, Germany, and the USA there was no change in death rates, despite increases in aerosol sales. Secondly the deaths all had the appearance of severe asthma, rather than an appearance suggesting heart damage due to the bronchodilator. Furthermore, the deaths were commonest in the very age group, ten to fourteen years, least likely to be subject to cardiac damage.

Was there a relationship between the deaths and the aerosols? The answer to this must almost certainly be 'no', if the relationship is considered in terms of drug toxicity. But there may be a subtler relationship. The immediate relief afforded by the aerosol bronchodilator may have lulled the asthmatic patient and his doctor into a false sense of security. On the fatal occasion the bronchodilator was used several times with little effect. The attitude 'it will work better next time,' was adopted. But it did not, and before long the asthma attack had escalated to a severity that was unrelievable. With the awareness of this danger, deaths have decreased again although sales of bronchodilators, admittedly the selective ones, are now as high as in 1966.

In recent years a great deal has been learned about the action of bronchodilator drugs on chemical processes within the muscle cell. The details of this biochemistry are complex and it suffices to have a general idea of what is going on. Muscle contraction and relaxation are brought about by changes in the balance of chemicals within the muscle cells. These chemicals are in a state of flux, being formed, used, and destroyed constantly. Adrenaline, and the other sympathomimetic drugs discussed so far, act by accelerating the production of chemicals which encourage relaxation. Relaxation can also be encouraged by preventing the breakdown of these same chemicals. This end can be achieved by using drugs of a different type. The general chemical name for such drugs is the methylxanthines. Caffeine in coffee and tea is closely related to these compounds. Though it has only a small effect on bronchial muscle, it does have the very useful stimulant action of many sympathomimetic drugs on the flagging brain. Legend has it that the stimulant action of coffee was discovered by an Arabian prior. Learning from the local shepherds that goats which had eaten berries from the coffee plant gambolled and frisked all through the subsequent night, the prior copied them to help him maintain his vigil through long nights of prayer.

The drug in this group best known to asthmatics is aminophylline. Like adrenaline, aminophylline is most dramatically effective when injected. Unlike adrenaline it is best given directly into a vein. It does have a stimulant action on the heart, and is always injected slowly. Given in this way, aminophylline has long since superceded adrenaline as the preferred treatment for acute asthmatic attacks. It is now being rivalled by salbutamol by injection, but so far there seems little to

Bronchodilators

choose between them. Aminophylline is not injected under the skin or into the muscles: that would be painful.

Aminophylline cannot be prepared in a form suitable for inhalation so that for more routine use aminophylline is taken by mouth. Pure aminophylline irritates the stomach: nausea and sickness are the results. So the pharmaceutical companies have adopted two approaches to make it more pleasant to take. The first has been to alter it chemically to lessen the gastric disturbance, yet retain its effect on the bronchial muscle. Silbephylline and proxyphylline are examples. The second has been to change the way in which aminophylline itself is made into tablet form. Besides being more palatable these preparations are also slow-release in type. As with the slow release salbutamol, they give benefit for ten to twelve hours, and so can be taken twice daily. Theograd and Phyllocontin are two examples of slow-release aminophylline preparations.

Aminophylline can be given by another route: rectally as a suppository. The distaste with which some might view using a medicine by this route, is socially and racially determined. The French favour it for many types of medicine. And when the asthmatic has experienced the quick relief that an aminophylline suppository can give, his taboos are soon overcome.

So what is the place of aminophylline and similar drugs in relation to the selective beta 2 stimulant bronchodilators. They are a second line of defence. They seem to smooth out some of the sharp jags in the swinging asthmatic process. Taken before going to bed, the slow release tablets or a suppository will often protect against bothersome early morning wheezing. During the day their influence can add to the effect of the inhaled bronchodilator rather than replacing it. The injection of aminophylline is still preferred by most doctors for treating the sharp attack of asthma.

Mention needs to be made now of certain tablets and capsules which contain more than one bronchodilator. The best known are probably Amesec, Franol, and Tedral. All contain an adrenergic type sympathomimetic, ephedrine: and an aminophylline type of agent, theophylline. Because of the stimulant action of ephedrine on the brain, they also contain a sedative, phenobarbitone. Now, whilst it is sometimes necessary to give a second drug to counteract the unwanted side effects of another useful agent, this can only really be justified if there is no alternative to the useful agents. This is no longer true as far as ephedrine is concerned. Mixtures such as these are therefore rather frowned upon. It is especially important that the elderly be dissuaded from using

119

UK approved names	UK trade names	Other approved names	Other trade names
ACEPIFYLLINE	*Etophylate*	ACEFYLLINE PIPERAZINE	*Etaphylline (Aus)*
AMINOPHYLLINE	*Cardophylin, Phyllocontin, Theodrox*	AMINOPHYLLINUM (IP)	*Aminodur (US) Carine (Aus)*
BAMIFYLLINE	*Trentadil*		
CHOLINE THEOPHYLLINATE	*Choledyl*	OXTRIPHYLLINE (US)	
DIPROPHYLLINE	*Neutraphylline, Silbephylline*	DIHYDROXYPROPYL-THEOPHYLLINUM (Aus)	*Dyflex Neothylline* } *(US)*
ETAMIPHYLLINE	*Millophylline*		
METHOXYPHENAMINE	*Orthoxine*		
PROXYPHYLLINE	*Brontyl, Thean*	PROXIPHYLLINUM (IP)	
THEOPHYLLINE	*Aminomed, Englate, Labphylline Monotheamin, Nuclin Rona-Phyllin Theograd*	THEOPHYLLINUM (IP)	*AB Elixir (Aus) Bronkodyl (US) Theo-Dur (US)*

IP = International Pharmacopoeia   US = United States of America   Aus = Australia

Fig. 28. A list of methylxanthine bronchodilators in common use.

Bronchodilators

preparations containing ephedrine because of the very adverse effects it can have on bladder emptying. One word in mitigation must be said. If a patient has been established on a particular, and for them effective, remedy over many years, it is often best to leave the status quo. The reason is that the potential increased benefit from the new agent, must be carefully balanced against the importance of psychological reliance on a known and trusted remedy.

It was noted earlier that the parasympathetic division of the autonomic nervous system excites responses in the organs it serves, which are in general opposite or complementary to those of the sympathetic nervous system. Stimulation of the vagus nerve, the parasympathetic nerve to the lungs, causes contraction of bronchial muscle. Through the activity of this nerve the normal bronchial muscle is kept 'toned up': without it, the smaller bronchi might simply collapse. Additional tone is engendered through the vagus nerve by reflex activity as described earlier. Such reflex activity is important in causing brief episodes of chest tightness. The activity of these reflexes can be dampened down by blocking the effect of the parasympathetic neurotransmitter, acetylcholine, on the bronchial muscles. The drug that achieves this is atropine.

Like ephedrine, atropine has a long history. It is extracted from the plant *Atropa belladona*. The name has a lurid derivation. In Greek mythology Atropos was one of the three fates who cut with shears the web of life woven by her sisters Clotho and Lachesis. Atropine has been used as a poison. Dilute extracts of the plant were at one time fashionable as eye drops to dilate the pupils, hence 'belladonna'. As a herbal remedy it has had an established place in the Indian subcontinent for over 4000 years. It was recommended that the leaves be smoked in a pipe till 'the chest, throat, and head become light, and the cough reduced'. Brought to this country through British Army physicians stationed in India in the last century, it has had a rather chequered history, falling in and out of favour.

The recent renewed interest in atropine as a bronchodilator, has arisen as a result of animal experiments. In attempts to understand asthma, animal models have been created. Both dogs and monkeys will develop allergic asthma. Challenge tests with the appropriate antigen will predictably result in an asthmatic episode. Administering atropine will, in these animals, prevent the antigen challenge inducing asthma. Challenge studies have also been carried out in man. Here the effect of atropine is controversial. Protection against the challenge has sometimes been recorded, but in other studies no effect could be found.

In practice the benefits to be obtained from the use of atropine in

121

Bronchodilators

asthma turn out to be limited. Atropine will block reflex activity in the vagus nerve, but the sympathomimetic drugs have an identical effect. This is because the end result of the reflex is muscle contraction —and the sympathomimetic drugs relax the muscle. Furthermore when the activity of atropine is compared directly with that of sympathomimetic drugs such as isoprenaline or salbutamol in asthmatics, it is found to be less effective. This is in striking contrast to the effect obtained in patients with chronic bronchitis causing narrowing of the airways. In such patients atropine is at least as effective as the beta 2 stimulants in relaxing the obstruction, and sometimes more effective. In a given individual there is often a mixture of factors leading to airways obstruction. Cigarette smoking and infection lead to bronchitis; heredity and allergy lead to asthma. The more features of allergy that are detectable, the less will be the response to atropine. That it is the allergic component to the airways narrowing that is resistant to the action of atropine, in man, is illustrated by the fact that after the allergic component has been treated any residual airways narrowing will now respond to atropine.

In conclusion, bronchodilators represent the foundation stone of therapy in bronchial asthma. They relieve the tightness and wheezing caused by narrowed airways. They can be used prophylactically to anticipate situations likely to provoke asthma. Overwhelmingly the best way to deliver a bronchodilator is by the aerosol route. Tablets may be substituted if the asthmatic seems unable to use an inhaler, or in slow release form before retiring to bed to maintain bronchodilator activity through the night. Aminophylline as a tablet or suppository, also comes into this second category, and this agent is the first choice of the doctor for injection in a sharp attack.

11

The place of steroids

ATTITUDES towards steroid therapy amongst doctors and patients alike have become polarized. The patient either swallows steroid tablets like sweets, or refuses to have 'those dreadful tablets again'. One doctor will leave a supply in the patient's home; another will refuse to prescribe except in dire emergency. What are steroids and why is there so much controversy about their use?

The word steroid, in scientific terms, refers to a large group of substances having a common structure. In medical terms most steroids of interest are hormones. The sex hormones are steroids. So are hormones from the outer surface of the adrenal gland, the adrenal cortex. These are given the name corticosteroids. Corticosteroids are essential to life. Without them, as Addison described in 1855, the body wastes away and the blood pressure cannot be maintained. Extracts of the adrenal cortex were purified during the 1930s and the individual steroids identified. Of most general interest are cortisone and the closely related hydrocortisone. The production of these hormones by the adrenal gland is under the direction of another hormone, adrenocorticotropic hormone (ACTH) secreted by the pituitary, a gland which nestles in the depths of the skull, underneath the brain.

Throughout the 1940s there was intense interest in discovering the natural role of the adrenal corticosteroid hormones. Hans Selye pioneered the notion that they were concerned with the body's response to stress. Acting through the brain, stress causes an outpouring of ACTH, which in its turn stimulates corticosteroid output by the adrenal glands. Many illnesses, he pointed out, were accompanied by so-called non-specific symptoms which most physicians ignored; tiredness, listlessness, loss of appetite, and so forth. Selye argued that these symptoms arose because of maladaptation of the pituitary/adrenal system.

Complementary to this train of thought was the observation that during pregnancy, when many steroid hormones are produced by the body, patients with arthritis often experienced relief from their joint pains. Against this background Hench tried giving cortisone to a patient with acute rheumatoid arthritis. The result was dramatic. The impact of this discovery on medicine can be gauged by noting that a year later,

The place of steroids

in 1950, Hench and the chemists who had isolated and purified cortisone, received the Nobel prize for Medicine.

Soon cortisone was being tried in a wide variety of conditions with varying but often striking success. One of these conditions was asthma. It was very quickly evident that steroids would combat severe life-threatening attacks of asthma. Disappointing relapses then began to appear when the steroids were withdrawn and before long it emerged that long-term maintenance treatment was essential in some patients. This policy brought with it the spectre of slowly progressive and potentially serious side effects, which caused something of a reaction against the use of steroids in the 1960s. The pendulum has now swung back to a more sensible position, partly due to the skills learned from experience, partly due to the introduction of steroids in aerosol form.

Surprisingly little is known about the way in which steroids produce their beneficial effects in asthma. Whilst this in no way limits their use as an effective treatment, it does represent a failure in understanding that could have important implications. It will shortly become apparent that the use of steroids is limited by their tendency to produce unwanted side effects. It is quite possible that those portions of the steroid molecule that are responsible for the beneficial effects in asthma, are not the same as those causing the side effects. If this were indeed so, the way would be opened up for devising new steroids which retain the beneficial effects but lack the side effects.

Two facts are known which help a little in understanding the action of steroids in asthma. First, steroids protect against allergy; not against immediate allergy but against the later reaction. Thus with aspergillus mould or one of the occupational allergens described in Chapter 8, the reaction at four to six hours can be prevented by a dose of steroids prior to challenge with the allergen. Secondly, though steroids are not bronchodilators, they do help bronchodilators to be more effective. In the severe asthmatic giving a corticosteroid together with salbutamol is better than giving salbutamol alone.

Not long after the introduction of the natural corticosteroids, which were extracted from the adrenal glands of animals, it became possible to manufacture corticosteroids in the laboratory. The aim, as so often in pharmaceutical research, has been to eliminate side effects and improve the beneficial effects. This has not been as successful with steroids as with some other drugs. The main achievement has been to make the manufactured steroids more powerful weight for weight than the natural corticosteroids. This has been accompanied by a slight emphasis in favour

UK approved names	UK trade names	Other approved names	Other trade names
BECLOMETHASONE	Becotide (Aerosol)		Aldecin (Aus)
BETAMETHASONE	Betnelan, Betnesol, Bextasol (Aerosol)	BETAMETHASONUM (IP)	Celestone (Aus : US)
CORTISONE	Cortelan, Cortistab, Cortisyl		Cortate (Aus) Cortone (US)
DEXAMETHASONE	Decadron, Dexacortisyl, Oradexon	DEXAMETHASONUM (IP)	Dexone (US) Dexmethsone (Aus)
HYDROCORTISONE	Efcortelan, Efcortisol, Hydrocortistab Hydrocortone, Solu-cortef	CORTISOL	Eldecort (US) Cetacort (Aus)
METHYL-PREDNISOLONE	Depo-medrone, Medro-cortex Medrone,Solu-medrone		Medrol (Aus : US)
PARAMETHASONE	Haldrate, Metilar		
PREDNISONE and PREDNISOLONE	Codelcortone, Codelsol, Decortisyl Delta cortril, Delta-cortef, Deltacortone Deltastab, Di-adreson, Precortisyl Prednesol, Sintisone, Ultra cortenol	PREDNISO(LO)NUM (IP)	Deltasolone (Aus) Prelone (Aus) Meticortelone (US)
TRIAMCINOLONE	Adcortyl, Kenalog Ledercort, Lederspan		Triamacin (US) Kenalone (Aus)

IP = International Pharmacopoeia   US = United States of America   AUS = Australia

Fig. 29. A list of corticosteroids in common use.

125

The place of steroids

of the effects thought likely to be most beneficial in treating illnesses, and against some of the side effects.

Whilst a large number of steroids have been manufactured, a very few need to be mentioned in the context of the treatment of asthma. Chief amongst these is prednisone or the very closely related, prednisolone (prednisone is in fact converted into prednisolone in the body). Prednisone is the agent most commonly used when prescribing corticosteroid therapy by mouth. When injections are required, the natural corticosteroid, hydrocortisone is the one usually chosen. The recently introduced steroid aerosols were specifically synthesized so that whilst they have a powerful action locally, they are poorly absorbed. The two used for this purpose are beclomethasone and betamethasone.

Tested in a laboratory setting, a single dose of prednisone will produce detectable relief in an asthmatic in about three hours though its maximum effect is not evident for about nine hours. When used in practice a course of prednisone tablets rather than a single dose is used. For many attacks of asthma a sequence of six 5mg prednisone tablets the first day, followed by five the next, four the day after and so on, is perfectly adequate. It is short, sharp, beneficial, and does not, over this six-day period, produce side effects. Indeed a course like this can be repeated several times a year, if necessary, wihout ill effect. Sometimes a longer course is required, generally when the attack is more severe. It may be initiated with an injection of hydrocortisone. If more intensive steroid treatment seems indicated, hospital will be the place for it to be carried out. Repeated injections of hydrocortisone are used and a course of prednisone prescribed to follow, which will start with a larger initial dose and continue for longer, perhaps three or four weeks.

The pattern of recommended dosage after an acute attack will vary from patient to patient, but the aim all the time will be a gradual paring away at the dose until the prednisone can be stopped altogether. In a few instances, unacceptable wheeziness returns within a few days of stopping the prednisone or even before it has been stopped. This is when the difficult decision about long-term maintenance steroid therapy has to be made. Steroids have a bad, and not unjustified, record of causing ill health through side effects: but always a careful balance must be struck between intolerable disability due to the asthma and the possibility of even inevitability of side effects. Chronic asthmatics can often be kept in very good health on a dose of prednisone between 5 and 10mg each day. At this level even after many years, side effects are minimal and mostly not serious. Side effects become more likely if the dose is raised very much above 10mg per day.

The place of steroids

Because there is, rightly, concern about the side effects of steroids, it is worth having some idea of the frequency with which they can be expected.

The most obvious unwanted effect of taking corticosteroids for any length of time is a gain in weight. This is partly attributable to an interference with the way in which the body handles foodstuffs. Much of the weight gain is due to the laying down of fat especially around the trunk and on the face, and it becomes obvious in about one third of asthmatics taking continuous corticosteroids for more than a year. Some half of these also show evidence of swelling of the ankles, suggesting that part of the weight gain is due to retention of fluid in the body. With fluid retention there is often a rise in blood pressure, though this is likely in less than one in ten. Two other important side effects appear in about a sixth of those asthmatics requiring continuous corticosteroids for more than a year—these are indigestion sufficient to lead to a definite stomach ulcer, and thinning of the bones sufficient to lead to a fracture. Few asthmatics require continuous steroids for this long and if courses are given intermittently over the same period then the frequency with which these more dramatic side effects are seen is cut to about a quarter.

Corticosteroid treatment interferes with certain internal defence mechanisms against infection and the stress of injury. Many asthmatics experience some change of mood on corticosteroid therapy. In the doses required by most, this is rarely serious and is more likely to be an elevation in mood rather than a depression. Thinning of the skin and easy bruising are common in the elderly requiring maintenance corticosteroids. In children the commonly seen weight gain is made rather more obvious by a retardation in height gain.

There is one additional long-term effect which is an inevitable consequence of continuous steroid therapy. This is the suppression of the adrenal glands' normal response to stress. In health the adrenal glands naturally produce a quantity of cortisone equivalent to about 5 to 10mg of prednisone a day. If prednisone in this dose is being taken each day, its properties are so equivalent to the natural hormone that the adrenals no longer need to manufacture their own cortisone. This dose is not however adequate for times of stress—the stress of a road accident, an operation, an infection, even an acute attack of asthma. Normally the adrenal glands would respond to these stresses by pouring out more cortisone, but if their manufacturing processes have been suppressed for months on end because prednisone has been taken, they cannot respond quickly enough to the demands placed on them. Indeed sometimes they cannot respond at all.

The place of steroids

This problem has important implications when it comes to altering steroid doses. The natural history of asthma is such that there are times of life when asthma, in a given individual, is bothersome, and others when it is less so. Maintenance prednisone therapy instituted in a time of severe asthma may later become unnecessary. But prednisone cannot, must not, be stopped abruptly. If it is, the adrenal glands will have insufficient cortisone reserves even for everyday life. Given time, they will recover. During this time the dose of prednisone will need to be reduced very slowly, perhaps by as little as a 1mg reduction in the total daily dose of prednisone each month. This very gradual tailing down, will enable the ACTH produced naturally by the pituitary gland in response to stress, to exert its control over the dormant adrenal cortex once more. It was thought at one time that injections of ACTH might hasten this process, but in fact this is not so. The injected ACTH merely suppresses a stage further back in the sequence. Now the pituitary becomes lazy and will not respond naturally to stress.

ACTH is occasionally used as an alternative to oral prednisone tablets. It acts by stimulating the adrenal glands to produce excessive quantities of natural corticosteroids. The fact that it needs giving by injection is regarded by the majority as a distinct disadvantage. Very often, however, once or twice weekly injections are sufficient, and the occasional patient seems to respond better to ACTH than to prednisone. Claims have been made that in adults ACTH is safer than prednisone, and that in children it causes less retardation in growth. The evidence in favour of these benefits is not firm, and most physicians would now use steroid aerosols as an alternative to prednisone rather than ACTH.

An attempt to administer steroids directly to the lungs of asthmatics was made in the early days of corticosteroid manufacture. Unfortunately all the initial steroids were highly soluble so that they were absorbed into the body equally readily whether given by inhalation or swallowed. This meant that as far as side effects were concerned, the inhalation route offered no advantage, and therapeutically both routes were equally effective.

Steroids were subsequently found to be an effective treatment for several skin conditions. For these, steroid creams or ointments were spread over large areas of skin, and a great deal was absorbed. Side effects were a great problem. Research was therefore directed towards finding steroids that were locally very powerful, but being insoluble, were absorbed very poorly. Betamethasone and beclomethasone were two such steroids which resulted from this research. Having solved this problem for the skin, attention was directed once again to the lungs.

128

The place of steroids

The two steroids were prepared in aerosol form and introduced for the treatment of asthma in 1969, beclomethasone being Becotide and beta-methasone, Bextasol.

The steroid aerosols have made a valuable contribution to the management of moderately severe asthma. They are employed exclusively as a long-term maintenance therapy and must be given at least twice and preferably three or four times daily. Because all other pressurized aerosols are bronchodilators, there has been an unfortunate tendency for patients to regard the steroid aerosols in this light. If they do, they will be disappointed. Steroid aerosols do not give the immediate relief produced by bronchodilators, and their true worth only emerges with continuous use. They have two roles. First, they can entirely replace small doses of maintenance prednisone. Used regularly with a bronchodilator they keep many moderately troubled asthmatics free of wheezing. Secondly they can partly replace oral prednisone in those who do require it regularly in larger doses. Thus with the addition of a steroid aerosol four times daily, it may be possible to maintain the same level of control over the asthma with 6mg of prednisone daily rather than, say 10mg daily. There will be a consequent reduction in the likelihood of side effects from the oral prednisone.

Steroids, wherever administered, might be expected to cause some trouble. Fortunately the side effects from aerosol steroids have not been too serious. Hoarseness is the commonest complaint. It is usually due to a chemical inflammation of the larynx. Sometimes there is an infection with a yeast-like fungus called candida. The infection is usually evident in the back of the throat and on the palate where it causes the white patches that give it its common name, thrush. Candida infection causes an unpleasant sore throat and whilst it can be treated with antifungal lozenges, and may be helped by reducing the dose of steroid aerosol, thrush is the commonest reason for having to stop the steroid aerosol. Steroids continually rubbed into the skin cause it to become thin and vulnerable to injury. Fortunately there is no evidence yet (after three or four years' experience), that the same problem will occur in the throat or bronchi.

If you are on corticosteroids, you should carry a 'Steroid Card' with you, which gives details of your treatment. You could also wear a Medic-Alert disc on a bracelet or neck chain*. If you are unfortunate enough to be involved in an accident, if you need an operation, or if you develop certain acute illnesses, you may need more corticosteroid

*The Medic-Alert Foundation, 9 Hanover Street, London, W1R 9HF.

The place of steroids

treatment than that necessary just to control your asthma. The attending doctor will know what to give by reference to your steroid card. Finally *never* stop corticosteroid treatment abruptly. It is unwise to make sudden changes in any of the treatment used in asthma, but it can be positively dangerous suddenly to reduce drastically or stop corticosteroid treatment.

12

Prevention

WHATEVER differences of opinion might exist about the treatment of asthma, all agree that ideally asthma should be prevented. The tendency to asthma, it has been seen, is to some degree hereditary. Whilst inherited characteristics cannot be altered it might be possible to modify their expression. Though the degree to which this is feasible may be limited, the efforts that have been made to achieve this goal deserve careful appraisal.

The irritable airways of the asthmatic are influenced by a variety of triggers. Control can be exercised over some of these. Environmental temperature changes, fumes, fog and similar irritants can be avoided up to a point. Infections can be reduced by taking evasive action. Psychological stresses may be amenable to resolution. But the possibilities for environmental control are focused most sharply on the question of allergens. The responsibility of industry for the environmental control of industrial allergens has already been pointed out. Cats, dogs, and horses can be banished: plants can be thrown out, specific foods avoided. Pollen exposure can be cut down by staying indoors or living in a town. Success is not by any means assured, largely because the very presence of allergens in the atmosphere seems to set up a state of airways irritability. Wheezing on exercise, at night or in response to irritants is as much part of allergic asthma as is any direct response to mowing the lawn, dusting the house or handling pets.

Perhaps more effort has been put into reducing the dust load in the homes of children with dust mite allergy, than any other form of environmental allergen control. What is involved? Since the mite congregates wherever there are warm humid conditions and human skin scales, it will predominate in bedrooms, in cushions, on carpets. A rigorous routine would involve; vacuuming the mattress, especially under the buttons and piping, every other day; keeping the bedroom dry; and wiping all flat surfaces with a damp cloth at least once a week. The bedclothes should be shaken outside, whenever possible, and washed frequently. Feather pillows, eiderdowns, and woollen blankets should be replaced by others of synthetic material. Carpets and heavy textured curtains should be avoided. A certain amount of household dust can be removed from the atmosphere by the use of air conditioners.

Prevention

They have to fight a constant battle against draughts and the opening of doors and windows. Furthermore, the chief culprit, the house dust mite hides in bedding from which it is not easily extracted.

Is it all worthwile? In many instances parents and doctors have been convinced that dust control has made a significant difference to the asthmatic symptoms of individual children. Disappointingly, comparisons of the progress of one group of children in whose homes dust control has been carried out, with another group where no such measures have been adopted, reveal no differences. For such an amount of hard work to be worthwhile, the impact on the asthma should be really obvious. If house dust mite sensitivity is such an important feature in childhood asthma, why have the results of dust control been so negative? Partly because control has to be almost inhumanly rigorous to reduce the mite load to negligible proportions, and partly because, even when skin testing and bronchial provocation suggest house dust mite allergy to be important, there are in fact many other trigger factors. The loss of one trigger might not make a detectable difference to the overall pattern and frequency of asthmatic episodes in that child.

A similar question arises in relation to household pets. Should the family cat, dog, guinea-pig, or whatever be sacrificed? In the very few instances where an animal allergy is the only cause for asthma the answer is clear enough. Very often however it is only one allergy amongst many. Before making any decision that would cause distress, some sort of trial separation must be engineered. Holidays away from home and animals are the most convenient way of arranging this, but not the most ideal. The lack of the cat or dog is only one of the many environmental changes that take place, and possibly the least important. It is better to arrange for the animal to be put into kennels whilst the child stays at home and every other facet of the home environment is kept constant. Particles of animal hair and dander will lie around for some time in household dust so that the separation will need to be accompanied by a thorough cleaning programme. In the experience of most families, if animal allergy is only one amongst several triggers, then removal of the animal is, as with dust mite control, unlikely to be of great benefit.

More serious questions are raised when general environmental conditions seem to be implicated. Should the asthmatic consider moving house, district, country? In only a few instances will the answer be 'yes'. What evidence exists is largely circumstantial. Old damp houses near rivers do harbour more house dust mites: high altitude, dry, centrally-heated houses do not. How much of the relief of asthma, following

Prevention

the removal of children from low lying north western European countries to the Swiss Alps, was a result of environmental allergen change, is debatable. Damp houses also harbour moulds. Damp areas in general seem to be inimical to the asthmatic, whereas warm dry areas are favoured. The reputation of an area as a haven for patients with asthma can produce a bizarre distortion in the distribution pattern of disease. Arizona in the southern United states is such an area. The influx of chest sufferers to this state has resulted in a prevalence of chronic chest illnesses higher than anywhere else in North America.

Yet no area should be considered either right or wrong for asthmatics. Some will benefit from one set of environmental conditions, others from another. In most asthmatics, environmental conditions and allergens have such a small influence on their symptoms that moving house will have no effect at all. As with the pets, no decision should be made on moving until after a very careful and preferably prolonged trial period in the possible new location.

Hyposensitization

Hyposensitization—or desensitization as it is often incorrectly named—potentially offers a cure for asthma. It is extensively employed by specialists in allergy particularly in North America, but regarded with scepticism by others, especially physicians in Great Britain. For a method of treatment introduced as long ago as 1911, it is surprising and even reprehensible that there is so much doubt as at present exists about its efficacy.

Noon in 1911 thinking that pollen hayfever was due to a toxin given off by the pollen, argued that if antitoxin could be developed in the body then the hayfever could be treated. This he hoped to achieve by injecting first very dilute and then increasingly concentrated solutions prepared from extracts of grass pollen. It appeared to be effective and later the same year Freeman first reported that asthma accompanying summer hayfever was also ameliorated.

These injection programmes were developed before the allergic nature of hayfever had been formulated, but even when it became clear that toxins were not implicated, allergists persisted in using hyposensitizing injections. In recent years the theoretical background for giving these injections has been questioned and explored. It will be recalled (Chapter 4) that atopic allergy involves the production of specific IgE antibodies which attach themselves to mast cells. Injections of an allergen excite the production of IgG antibodies which circulate in the

133

Prevention

bloodstream. It has been suggested that these IgG antibodies latch onto inhaled allergens before they have a chance to get at the mast cell. Such a notion seems rather naive when it is realized that IgG in all probability cannot get to the airways where, almost certainly, the first encounter between allergen and mast cells takes place. It does appear however that after a series of hyposensitizing injections, less IgE is produced during the pollen season and sensitivity to histamine is reduced.

But are these dubious immunological changes accompanied by any benefit to the patient? Leaving aside asthma for a moment, there does seem no doubt that hyposensitizing injections given in late winter do benefit grass hayfever and ragweed sufferers the following summer. A single set of injections will not give much 'carry-over' effect in the following season and injections for three consecutive winters are generally recommended. After this, it is difficult to distinguish between relief due directly to the injections and spontaneous recovery which is such a feature of summer seasonal nose allergies. In a few subjects, repeated winter injections over many years do seem to be necessary and beneficial.

What of asthma? Here the picture is far from clear. Pollen asthma may appear to improve together with the hayfever but it may not, and asthmatic symptoms at other times of the year will be uninfluenced. Some studies do report quite high remission rates—for example improvement in 80 per cent—but control groups have not always been included, and when they have, a 40 per cent improvement is not uncommon.

Much effort has been expended into devising an injection course that will benefit sufferers from perennial asthma with evidence of house dust mite sensitivity. Studies that have used a proper control group, who are given injections of the solvent only with no dust component, began in the mid 1950s. Something like half the studies have suggested benefit, and half no effect. What can be gleaned from a careful analysis of these, is that hyposensitization for house dust allergy seems most likely to succeed, first, when the subjects are children, secondly when the symptoms are all the year round but obviously exaggerated in the presence of household dust, and thirdly when extracts of the house dust mite are used rather than crude dust extracts. When it has been assessed, bronchial sensitivity to mite extract has decreased after a course of injections.

Prophylaxis

The prevention of attacks of asthma by taking regular medication is

134

Prevention

rather different from prevention by environmental control or hypo-sensitizing injections, and is known as prophylaxis. It can be achieved using one of the most remarkable discoveries in asthma research of the past twenty years—disodium cromoglycate (DSCG: Intal). This drug was discovered in the early 1960s by Dr Roger Altounyan. He was investigating the properties of an Egyptian root from which an ancient remedy Khellin was derived. Khellin had been used for many years as a mild bronchodilator and for the relief of spasm in the bowel and kidney. Altounyan's contribution was to show that besides this property, Khellin contained a component which was not a bronchodilator but had antiallergic properties. The purified compound DSCG proved to be the most powerful agent discovered in this research programme. It was shown to have very specific antiallergic properties in immediate allergy. If given just before the inhalation of an allergen extract to which the subject was known to be sensitive, DSCG would protect against the airways, narrowing normally to be expected.

It did not bronchodilate. Its effect waned after four to five hours, and it proved to have no effect if given after the challenge. It was not absorbed from the stomach and had to be given by inhalation (Plate V). Given four times a day as a prophylactic agent in the clinical setting, it often gave some improvement within days. Its maximal effect however was not evident for several weeks. Over this time it had an increasingly beneficial effect, reducing wheezing and chest tightness and lessening the need for bronchodilators and steroids. Some difficulty was experienced in demonstrating that it improved lung function, but there seems no doubt that it does so.

Other interesting properties turned up on further study. DSCG afforded protection against exercise-induced asthma in about 60 per cent of children. It reduced the sensitivity of the asthmatic to histamine; it improved the asthmatic's response to atropine. Laboratory studies have revealed that all these activities appear to be due to a stabilizing effect of DSCG on the mast cell. In the presence of DSCG the mast cell no longer breaks up to release its damaging granules when exposed to allergen.

The patients who benefit most from DSCG are those who most clearly have atopic allergic asthma, and especially children. The response in adults is less predictable and there seems to be little or no protection against wheezing attacks precipitated by infection. In the atopic subject, DSCG is still the safest first choice after bronchodilators have failed to control symptoms. Side effects, apart from some irritation in the throat and a bitter flavour, are very uncommon.

135

Prevention

DSCG does not dissolve in the propellants used for the pressurized aerosols (e.g. for salbutamol and beclomethasone) and has to be given as a dry powder. This is whirled up into a cloud after puncturing the capsule in which it is supplied, using a specially designed device—the spinhaler. The particles clog together if the capsules become damp and the spinhaler must be kept clean. Despite these problems DSCG has now been in widespread use for over ten years and has made a very significant impact on both the management of asthma, and research into understanding the intricate cellular events that cause wheezing.

When bronchodilator and steroid therapy was under discussion, it was pointed out that every effort has been made to encourage aerosols rather than tablets. This was largely because of the unpleasant side effects of taking oral therapy. The position may be reversed in relation to antiallergic drugs such as DSCG which are used prophylactically. The reasons are complex. There is a certain inconvenience in using the spinhaler and it must be taken four times daily for adequate protection. Furthermore, if there are atopic manifestations in the nose, and eyes as well, separate preparations of DSCG must be applied to these sites. So the search has gone on for anti-allergic agents which can be taken by mouth, without causing troublesome side effects. These are early days yet. Several compounds have been tried and fallen by the wayside. Perhaps the most promising so far is ketotifen (Zaditen), which is taken as a capsule twice daily. It protects against allergen challenge as does DSCG; it compares with DSCG in clinical use, and it has a steroid-sparing effect. Time will tell whether it proves to have a useful place in the management of asthma.

13

Patterns of care

ASTHMA is pre-eminently a condition which can be managed by the patient (or his parents) under the guidance of the general practitioner. Being a common disorder every general practitioner will have experience in the care of asthma. Though much remains to be learned about the intimate mechanisms responsible for asthmatic wheezing, there is enough information available for every doctor to understand the principles of management. Furthermore, he should be able to tell the story of asthma sufficiently simply to enable his patients to undertake their day-to-day treatment without resorting to him for advice.

It is the family doctor who will first make the diagnosis. It is he who will distinguish asthma from wheezy bronchitis. He will be able to judge the importance of allergic triggers and emotional stresses. Inherited and environmental influences will be apparent to him because of his knowledge of the patient's family background. The general practitioner will initiate treatment. The mainstay will be bronchodilators, preferably by aerosol. He will be the one to demonstrate their use, to ensure that each patient has the technique mastered. He will explain how and when the aerosol is to be used: whether it is to be just for the occasional wheeze: whether it is to be used prophylactically or regularly.

The many asthmatics who have intermittent mild attacks will not see their general practitioner frequently. Once assured that the patient knows how to handle the bronchodilator, an occasional check up, repeat prescriptions, and a consultation when needed for sharp attacks will be the pattern of care.

Most general practitioners will appreciate the principles on which antiallergic therapy is based and will prescribe DSCG for the atopic asthmatic. Many are already familiar with the indication for the use of steroid aerosols. Asthmatics requiring these therapies are likely to be more bothered with symptoms than those requiring just bronchodilators and at least when such treatments are being started, more regular visits to the surgery will be necessary. But again the pattern of less frequent attendances is all that will be necessary when the use of these therapies has been established.

For sharp episodes of wheezing the general practitioner will leave instructions about increasing medication. For those of his patients

137

using corticosteroid therapy either intermittently or regularly, these instructions are likely to be fairly explicit, and he will most likely ask to be told when an increase in treatment has become necessary.

The capricious way in which asthma catches the patient unawares and produces a sharp episode of wheezing which may settle spontaneously or may progress to a more prolonged attack, leads very often to the question 'when do I call the doctor?' To offer advice to asthmatics about when to call the doctor is inviting criticism. The problems of one patient are never quite the same as those of another. Despite this, some general guidelines are not out of place, since for a condition that is as treatable as asthma, there are still too many hospital admissions and even deaths.

Most asthmatics expect a certain amount of variability in wheezing from moment to moment, or day to day—and so can recognize the sudden change that heralds a sharp attack. They will know which of the features described in Chapter 2 is peculiar to their particular brand of asthma. In a sharp attack the pulse rate rises. A rate above 110 per minute or the fading of the force of the pulse with breathing-in are signals to call in the doctor. Increasingly the peak flow machine* is being used at home by asthmatics to monitor progress. Different criteria of change will apply to different patients: it may be a sudden fall in peak flow by a specific amount, a drop below a critical level, or the failure of peak flow to rise in the evening above the figure obtained in the morning.

Bronchodilators should offer all asthmatics relief. If a bronchodilator fails to bring the relief expected, or any slight benefit is lost within half an hour then help from a doctor is needed.

A general practitioner visiting an asthmatic in a sharp attack at home will need to satisfy himself that his patient has correctly taken bronchodilators as aerosol or tablets. If these have failed to abate the attack, he will turn to injection therapy. Aminophylline is still probably the first choice. A single injection given slowly into a vein in the arm will begin to settle most attacks within ten to fifteen minutes. He might at the same time give some hydrocortisone into the same vein, if experience suggests that a course of steroids is likely to be necessary. Observation over about half-an-hour will generally be sufficient to judge whether the attack is settling. About one in ten acute attacks of asthma seen in this

---

*Mini-peak flow meters (see Plate I) are not available yet on the National Health Service in the UK though they ought to be. They cost about £10 each and some doctors now issue them to their patients.

way at home by general practitioners do not settle, and hospital admission becomes necessary.

Whilst the major responsibility for the care of asthma in the community rests with the family doctor, asthma is only one of a legion of problems with which he has to deal. He cannot be expected to have at his fingertips knowledge of every facet of the diagnosis and management of a single problem. So he may turn to the hospital physician. He may choose to refer the asthmatic to a hospital outpatient department for a variety of reasons. There may be some question mark over the diagnosis. Is this really asthma? Have I missed an allergy? In the adult, how much is smoking contributing? Or it may be that he is clear about the diagnosis and wants the reassurance of a specialist's opinion: perhaps more often wants his reassurance for the patient's sake, or with children, for the parents' sake. Fashions in treatment are constantly changing: new therapies are introduced. He may not be sure that he is using precisely the correct therapy for this particular asthmatic nor that he is using the correct dosage for maximal effect: so he asks for advice.

When referred, where can the asthmatic patients expect to be seen and by whom? The referral may be to a general medical clinic where the physician will have broadly based skills covering a wide range of medical problems. Very often the physician will be one with a special interest in chest problems. Chest physicians often work in chest clinics which are separate from the general hospital outpatients' department; and they may hold specialized clinics devoted to asthma. The hospital hierarchy consists of a consultant, a fully trained physician; registrars, doctors under going training to be hospital-based physicians; and housemen, the junior doctors serving their apprenticeship before branching out into a hospital career or going into training for general practice. A new outpatient with asthma will very often be seen by a consultant or a registrar: housemen are usually busy with ward duties.

What will be required of the asthmatic at an outpatient visit? Details of custom vary from one unit to another but most assessments will include essentially three steps before any sort of judgement is made or advice given: the taking of a history, an examination, and some sort of testing of lung function. The probing which takes place as the story of a patient's asthma is unfurled, may take him by surprise. Having read earlier chapters in this book, this should no longer be so. To the story of the evolution of his asthma from childhood will be added details of family history, occupation, pets, hobbies, holidays, and housing. The number of cigarettes smoked, social circumstances,

139

finances, worries, hopes, and expectations will all be taken into consideration in building up a complete picture of the asthmatic's life and illness.

A physical examination is an essential part of the assessment and so is some sort of objective measurement of lung function. Any of the tests mentioned in the second chapter of this book may be used, but most often it will be a peak expiratory flow rate or spirometry. If at the time of clinic attendance some asthma is present, the degree to which this can be immediately reversed with a bronchodilator aerosol will probably be checked. If there is no wheeze, more often in children, an immediate exercise test might be carried out to see if wheezing develops after exercise. Depending on a whole host of circumstances, other tests might be asked for: a blood test to look for anaemia—which can cause breathlessness—or for an indication of allergy: a chest radiograph to look for the changes that go with aspergillus asthma or to exclude other types of chest disease: and skin prick tests to evaluate atopic asthma.

The outcome of such a visit will vary according to the needs of the patient. Some advice may be given about life style, about the avoidance of allergens, about stopping smoking, about occupation. The physician may ask the asthmatic to chart day-by-day fluctuations in the amount of asthma he experiences by using a diary card (a typical example is shown in Fig. 30). These estimations of symptoms will usually be accompanied by some recordings of lung function at home with the simple portable peak flow machine. He may make some adjustments in therapy: changes in the type of bronchodilator and its dose or route of administration. If they have not been used previously, he may want to try the effect of DSCG or a steroid aerosol. With asthma that is poorly controlled, he may advise a course of prednisone by mouth. With any change of therapy he will almost always want a follow-up visit to judge the effect of his recommendations. He might ask the general practitioner to make further adjustments, so that the number of visits required will vary, partly with the requirements of the patient, partly with the approach of the physician, partly with the relationship between that physician and the patient's general practitioner. In a few instances especially where there are complex features in the causation of the asthma, where the condition has become chronic, where conventional treatment has been tried and failed, where there are other diseases complicating the issue, the family doctor will ask the hospital to keep a regular check on an asthmatic.

The hospital physician has resources to hand that are not available to the general practitioner. Apart from the investigative procedures

Patterns of care

Date of day of start / / 197	Days 1	2	3	4	5	6	7	Leave this column blank
(1) Night								
Good night 0								
Woken once by asthma 1								
Woken × 2–3 because of asthma 2								
Bad night, awake most of time 3								
(2) Day								
Symptom free 0								
Wheezy for an hour or two 1								
Wheezy for much of the day 2								
Wheezy all day 3								
(3) Peak flow gauge readings On waking in morning								
About 6 p.m.								
(4) Drugs in 24 hrs.								
Intal: No. of capsules inhaled								
Bronchodilator: No. of puffs (_____)								
Steroid aerosol: no. of puffs (_____)								
Prednisone: ____ total in mgs.								
Other (specify) _____								
(5) Comments Report anything unusual e.g. a cold								

Fig. 30. A diary card.

that he can carry out in lung function laboratories and the tests he can carry out for allergy, there is the question of admission to hospital. A spell in hospital may be necessary for one of three reasons. Firstly, because the asthma is so severe that hospital is the only safe place to treat it. Secondly, because it provides an environment where it is easy to make frequent adjustments to treatment and to monitor progress in doing so. And thirdly, because it provides facilities for investigating the precise cause of asthma.

Many sharp attacks of asthma to which the general practitioner is called, settle readily following one or two injections of aminophylline. There are many factors that the family doctor will take into consideration before recommending admission to hospital in an acute attack, but failure to respond to immediate treatment measures is one such.

The acutely ill asthmatic can expect to be the centre of attention on arrival in hospital. The procedures of assessment will be the same as those outlined for the outpatient visit but telescoped into a few minutes with the details omitted. An arterial blood sample will assess whether

141

oxygenation is impaired. Oxygen is likely to be given through a mask. A drip line will be fed into a vein for giving aminophylline or salbutamol as bronchodilators. Steroid therapy will be started with single doses of hydrocortisone given through a vein and maintained either with further doses intravenously or with tablets of prednisone.

Progress over the first few hours will be watched closely. Pulse rate, blood pressure, peak expiratory flow will be recorded, and the treatment schedule adjusted accordingly. Physiotherapists may be called in to help with coughing and relaxation. Additional bronchodilators may be given by aerosol—not using the pressurized cannisters but using a solution aerosolized into a mist. It is the policy in some units to deliver these solutions using devices which force air under pressure through the nebulizer. A breath in, or a button on the device will activate the delivery. The devices manufactured by the Bird and Bennet Companies are those commonly used in the United Kingdom (see Plates VI &VII).

Rarely, the immediate medication does not bring relief and the laboured breathing brings fatigue and exhaustion with the danger that breathing movement will become inadequate. Not only is oxygenation impaired but the carbon dioxide that should be eliminated by the lungs is retained in the body. This causes clouding of consciousness and eventual coma. Resort is made at this stage to artificial ventilation. The number of times this is required will not be more than a handful throughout the whole country each year—but when judiciously and appropriately applied, it is life saving.

It is the hospital's responsibility not only to treat acute severe asthma but also to investigate why it occurs, and why it is occasionally fatal. Reference has already been made to the 'epidemic' of deaths which occurred in the 1960s and which was thought, probably erroneously, to be due to the aerosol bronchodilators. Emphasis was lain at this time on the suddenness of these asthma deaths. There is always a small number of deaths due to asthma each year and a high proportion are reputedly sudden and unexpected. In England and Wales there are about a million asthmatics (2 per cent of the population) and just over 1000 deaths from asthma each year—this is only 0.002 per cent of the population. In the experience of any single physician an asthma death will fortunately be a rare event.

There are formidable difficulties in investigating the precise causes of these deaths. An attempt was made to look back over the deaths from asthma in the London area for the year 1971. Just under half occurred outside of hospital. In these patients there seemed to be a

Patterns of care

fairly uniform pattern. The small airways were not merely narrowed: they were blocked by thick sticky mucus, completely obstructing all flow of air. Of the deaths that occurred in hospital, only a few were truly unexpected, in the sense that they occurred in apparently well asthmatics. The remainder occurred in patients who had been admitted with severe asthma. Inadequate assessment or insufficient treatment were the most significant errors in the management of these patients.

Frequent recording of peak expiratory flow rates reveals that sharp attacks of asthma are most frequent in subjects who have a very marked variation between morning and evening values, and also in those whose values seem to vary in a haphazard and unpredictable way from day to day. Other patients especially at risk, are those who have recently reduced or stopped steroid therapy by mouth and whose adrenal glands are unable to respond to the stress of the acute attack by producing their own corticosteroids. All asthma deaths are certainly not explicable in the same way. Greater vigilance could, it seems, prevent some, but an unfortunate few will remain.

There is some suggestion that the prevalence of asthma is increasing. Running parallel with the increase in deaths from asthma in the 1960s was a rise in hospital admissions. The admission rate has stayed up, even though the death rate has fallen back to pre-1960 level. There is evidence too that the number of asthmatics attending general practitioner's surgeries has increased. In Birmingham, Dr Morrison-Smith has surveyed schoolchildren on three occasions in the past twenty years: the prevalence of asthma has risen from 1.8 to 6.3 per cent.

Patients admitted to hospital under less stressful circumstances will not be subjected to such urgent or vigorous treatment, as those admitted with an acute attack of asthma. If it is a question of adjusting treatment, careful measurements of function will be made, perhaps for several days, before making any changes. Such a procedure may well be adopted if steroid therapy is being considered for the first time. It may also be an occasion for trying out the effect of a newly introduced drug.

The investigation of mechanisms in asthma can take several forms. Sophisticated lung function testing can indicate the degree and extent of the airways' narrowing. Agents likely to provoke asthma may be tested for their effect on the airways' narrowing. This could be followed by evaluating therapeutic drugs for their ability to protect against such a challenge.

The hinterland between clinical management and research becomes blurred when mechanisms are being investigated or new drugs evaluated.

Patterns of care

The results will be pertinent to the management of the specific individual, but they also add to the body of information about mechanisms and therapy that will forward research in asthma. It should no longer be necessary for anyone to fear being a guinea-pig. Safeguards are wide ranging and carried out stringently. All new drugs have been exhaustively tested in experimental animals. They will be used cautiously in humans for short periods, before long-term trials in patients are undertaken. Careful blood checks are carried out and frequent clinical assessments made.

What questions are being asked in asthma research? A great deal of effort is expended in trying to discern the details of mechanism. Of the major trigger factors, much is known about allergy, but the classical atopic allergic reaction seems little in evidence in clinical asthma. Late reactions would seem to explain the clinical pattern of asthma much more satisfactorily but the number of common agents capable of exciting these reactions seems limited. Much mystery still surrounds the way in which infections trigger asthma and this field would seem one in which there is most to be learned. The importance of psychological triggers will continue to be debated for many years. If suggestion has such a powerful effect as that apparent in anecdotal observations and some carefully conducted studies, then the means of harnessing it and putting it to use need to be explored. It is still not clear whether irritability of the airways is the common underlying defect in all asthma, nor how this irritability comes about. The problem of heredity in asthma remains unsolved but its relevance in a therapeutic sense is questionable. New therapies are continually being put forward by the pharmaceutical companies. They require evaluation in clinical asthma. Some, like DSCG, contribute considerably to understanding the ways in which asthmatic wheezing is brought about.

14

Self-help and some words of advice

THE aim of this book has been to present the facts, in so far as they are known, about asthma. In doing so it is hoped that knowledge will dispel fear. An appreciation of the mechanisms which provoke attacks of asthma suggests steps which can be taken to avoid trigger factors. An understanding of the principles of the treatment of asthma allows the greatest benefit to be obtained from prescribed medicines. For the parents of an asthmatic child, knowledge can bring confidence in dealing with attacks, and regulating daily activity. Relieving a child's anxieties is halfway to allowing him to lead a normal and unrestricted life.

Many questions relating to the everyday management of asthma crop up which do not fall neatly into categories covered by previous chapters. This chapter therefore provides a miscellany of comment and advice that will go part way to filling in these omissions.

Relaxation

The asthmatic often asks how he can help himself in an attack. Any approach must centre on relaxation. The fear engendered by the approach, or the actual experience, of an attack of asthma causes tension. This tension is felt in the muscles around the neck, the shoulders, and even the arms and trunk. Whether it can also be reflected in tension in the muscles around the airways is not certain. Increasing tension does seem to escalate the distress caused by an asthma attack; and the relaxation of tension, to lessen it. Awareness of tension is the first step to relieving it. Each muscle group can be tensed and then deliberately relaxed. Techniques learned when the asthma is quiescent can be brought into use when an attack of wheezing develops. They enable the asthmatic, in some indefinable way, to cope with the attack.

The most sophisticated use of relaxation and muscle control is in Yoga. For those versed in these techniques, or willing and able to learn them, they offer an excellent way of providing relief from tension in an asthmatic attack, that will enable medications to have their optimal effect.

Self-help and some words of advice

Breathing Exercises

Beyond simple relaxation, comes the question of breathing exercises, taught by physiotherapists. There is probably no other aspect to the treatment of chest conditions that is as widely used, yet so unsupported by scientific study, as breathing exercises. It is not possible, save with the techniques of hypnosis, voluntarily to influence the muscle of the bronchi: only the voluntary muscles can be trained. The functions of the lung over which control can be exercised are therefore quite limited; the rate of breathing, the depth of breathing, and the relative contributions of various muscle groups to the movement of the chest. Even so, control cannot be complete. Any influence exercised over these muscles must bow to the overall requirement of breathing to match the amount of oxygen supplied to the oxygen needs of the body.

Deliberate alteration in the frequency with which breaths are taken is one of the more obvious ways in which voluntary control can be exercised over breathing. The rate of breathing seems to be capable of internal adjustment in the face of obstacles placed in the way of the free flow of air in and out of the lungs. In asthma the airways are narrowed. A moment's thought will reveal that more effort is going to be required to force air quickly through a narrow tube than to blow gently and slowly. It will thus be more economical of effort to breathe slowly and deeply through narrowed airways than it will be to breathe rapidly and shallowly. Some asthmatics find that they adopt this pattern naturally. Others, perhaps because of a sense of panic, seem to breathe more quickly than is really necessary, and become more distressed. The message to the asthmatic, then, is to breathe slowly.

A word of caution must be added. Slow breaths are usually deep breaths. It was once commonly taught that asthmatics should breathe out as much as possible: that they should empty their lungs with each breath. This encourages a forcing of the air out, and a compression of the lungs to a smaller size than they would reach at the end of a natural breath. This is wrong. It is wrong because it encourages not only compression of the lungs but compression too of the airways themselves, the very airways through which it is hoped to empty the lungs. Any additional force has the same effect. The force will be transmitted to the airways and will compress them. Relief will come if breathing is controlled at a slow rate with gentle breathing-out, allowing the lungs to relax down to a natural resting position but not forcing them beyond that.

There is agreement that relaxation and slow breathing are both

146

Self-help and some words of advice

beneficial and sound, in a scientific sense. Controversy surrounds the various techniques which claim to make it possible to move one part of the chest more than another. The muscles involved in breathing seem to fall into three groups: the diaphragm, the muscles between the ribs, and the muscles around the neck. The diaphragm is in use all the time. The outer muscles between the ribs assist breathing in and an inner layer of muscle pointing in the opposite direction, helps breathing out. According to the requirements of the body for air, just a few or very many rib muscles may be used. In the deep breathing of heavy exercise, the muscles around the neck and shoulders will help lift the chest. These groups of muscles are brought into use in sequence according to demand. When a call goes out for more air to be moved, it seems to be transmitted in a rather general way to the breathing muscles so that they respond according to an in-built pattern.

Conscious control over one group of muscles rather than another has been attempted. A deliberate raising of the upper part of the chest by contracting the muscles around the neck and shoulders is possible. A bigger breath in is the result. But the diaphragm also moves down more, even though no conscious effort is being directed towards it. It seems as though the muscles of breathing act 'all as a piece', and cannot be made to behave out of sequence. Elaborate exercises have been devised which purport to train one part of the chest—for example the left lower or upper right—to move independently of chest movements elsewhere. There is no evidence that any amount of training can achieve this aim.

Great emphasis has been lain on what has been called diaphragmatic breathing. The diaphragm is the dome-shaped muscle situated beneath the lungs. It is attached to the trunk all round its outer edge. When the muscle fibres in the diaphragm contract during breathing-in, the dome of the diaphragm moves downwards drawing the lungs with it. As it moves downwards, the diaphragm compresses the contents of the abdomen. It is natural for the muscles of the front wall of the abdomen to relax slightly during breathing-in so that this compression does not happen. Sometimes in asthma, this natural relaxation does not occur and these muscles may even be tightened in common with the tension developed in muscles elsewhere. This could restrict the downward movement of the diaphragm. The description 'diaphragmatic breathing' is given to the techniques whereby awareness of the movement of the front of the abdomen is heightened so that synchrony between the downward movement of the diaphragm with the forward relaxation of the abdominal wall can be achieved. Training will ensure

147

that this pattern is maintained when wheezing develops, and many asthmatics find it beneficial.

Diaphragmatic breathing is not really 'diaphragmatic'; it is abdominal. Conscious control is being exercised over the muscles of the abdominal wall, not the diaphragm. This does not detract from its value to patients, but it does emphasize that conscious control over diaphragmatic movement does not seem possible.

There is one theoretical objection to this technique. It becomes a practical reality only in the severest asthmatic attacks. In severe asthma the lungs become 'blown up'. The diaphragm is pushed down permanently by the overinflated lungs so that it is almost flat. Now, when its fibres contract, instead of lowering of the dome, drawing the lungs down, there will simply be a retraction inwards of the sides of the chest. Under these circumstances the diaphragm would work better if it could be made more domed. This might be possible by deliberately pushing the abdominal wall inwards. In practice some asthmatics do find relief in very severe attacks by doing this. It is not a technique that merits learning for the asthmatic, but it is worth noting that in very severe asthma, diaphragmatic/abdominal breathing techniques are likely to be somewhat less helpful to the asthmatic than at other times.

Helping the asthmatic child through an attack

'What should I do when he can't get his breath?' asks the mother of an asthmatic child. Perhaps the first rule is to remain calm yourself. Wheezing provokes anxiety and the child hates being at the mercy of his asthma. If your child senses that you are panicking, that you are uncertain what to do, his anxiety will be compounded.

Ensure that whatever medicines you have been advised to give in an attack, are given properly. This is especially true of inhalers. If the child is too distraught to synchronize the firing of his inhaler with breathing in, then do it for him. Watch him breathing in and out through the open mouth. Press the inhaler just as he begins to breathe in. Tell him to breathe right in and hold his breath for a moment. There is a magic about inhaling. Reinforce it with reassuring words and its effect will be doubled.

Make him comfortable: sitting in a chair, on the edge of the bed— often leaning forwards slightly. Encourage him to relax and breathe slowly. Remind him of breathing exercises he has been taught and make sure he uses them. He needs something to occupy his mind—anything will do. What you choose depends on your child—TV, a record, a story read aloud, a puzzle. All the time emphasis will be on an outward quiet confidence and an inward alertness. Calm does not mean carelessness, for, as described in the last chapter, there are signs to look for that suggest whether or not the doctor should be called.

Schooling

The parents of an asthmatic child face two decisions in relation to schooling. One is the immediate daily decision—should their child go to school on this particular day? The other is the long-term decision about special schooling.

It is impossible to make rules on day-to-day management that will apply to all asthmatic children. The individual decision will depend to a large extent on some index of severity. A child who has been awake half the night coughing and wheezing is generally in no fit state to go to school the next day. If a cold has led to wheezy bronchitis and the phlegm is turning yellow, it is probably best to keep the child at home and start treatment with an antibiotic. Each mother will have her own clues: the speed and ease with which washing, dressing, and eating breakfast are completed, the sallow look, the tinge of blueness in the lips, the pitch of the wheeze. Some will be using the portable peak flow meter and will have been advised of the significance of changes in the recorded flows. She will know too how to set these criteria against the whims and manipulations of her child. Is homework complete? Is there a disliked lesson on this day? Is it games day? She will find it less easy to look objectively at the way in which having her child home will impinge on her planned daily routine. She may be a working mother. How will the boss react to another day off work? In the end all these, sometimes conflicting, forces will result in a decision. There is no point in arguing afterwards whether that decision was right or wrong, such value judgements are irrelevant. The parent and child have come to terms with the asthma and the way one family lives with it, will not be the same as the way another would cope.

The decision about special schooling will be made with more deliberation and a good deal more heart searching. A very few children with asthma fall into this category—but the few that do, need special attention. The asthma will need to be severe and continuous with much time lost from ordinary school before the issue is raised. Most of the children will be on continuous steroid therapy. Consideration will be given to factors besides the severity of the asthma. Will parent/child separation be harmful, or is conflict in this relationship an important

149

facet in perpetuating the child's asthma? Is there a school near enough to make day attendance feasible—or will it mean boarding away from home? Do the educational facilities of the school match up to the requirements of the child? If expense is involved can this be provided by the parents, by the social services or by a charitable trust? The decision to send a child to a special school will not be made lightly, and ultimately the decision lies with the child and his parents though advice may come from many quarters.

Exercise and sport

Exercise is not harmful to the asthmatic. It very often is annoying and frustrating not to be able to engage in vigorous sporting activities because of shortness of breath: but it is not harmful. Indeed, physical fitness is as beneficial to the asthmatic as it is to anyone else.

The special problem of the wheezing that follows exercise must be faced in children, and less commonly in adults. It will be recalled that some six to eight minutes continuous running is required to induce post-exercise asthma. Athletic sports and games such as tennis which necessitate this degree of activity are therefore least well tolerated. Games such as football or cricket in which short bursts of activity are punctuated by spells of relative inactivity are ideal for the asthmatic. Most asthmatics enjoy swimming in which the water takes the weight of the body. Indeed, Olympic medals have been won for swimming by asthmatics. In relatively long distance running, the asthmatic teenager or adult may find he can 'run through' the wheezy spell by keeping going at a steady, gentle trot.

Most important of all, much of the terror of exercise-induced asthma can be obviated by prophylactic medication. Some children plan one of their doses of DSCG to fall just before the afternoon games session at school. DSCG is not effective in all children with exercise-induced asthma. A couple of puffs from a bronchodilator aerosol such as salbutamol is almost invariably protective. A bronchodilator will also relieve the wheezing should it come on, but anticipation with a dose before the game starts, is better.

A form of exercise specifically of the lungs themselves is the playing of wind instruments. The question is often raised whether this is harmful to the asthmatic. There is no evidence that it is. The control that playing a wind instrument teaches over the muscles of breathing could indeed be beneficial.

Self-help and some words of advice

Occupation

For the majority of asthmatics there needs to be little restriction on occupation. There are three important considerations when choosing a career. First, if specific allergies are known to exist, an occupation exposing the asthmatic to these allergens is obviously to be avoided. Those sensitive to dog hair should not become kennel maids: those sensitive to pollen should not become gardeners. Secondly, it would seem sensible that whatever their known trigger mechanisms, asthmatics should not enter occupations in which some specific occupational asthma has been reported (see Chapter 8). Thirdly the asthmatic who is persistently short of breath will clearly have to set aside occupations in which a lot of physical work is necessary.

Asthma developing in middle life may raise the question of changing jobs. The same considerations apply. A change nearly always means a change for the worse financially. It is therefore wise to ensure all the appropriate treatments have been explored before coming to an irrevocable decision.

Disability

Very few asthmatics become permanently disabled. Disability is essentially the total impact of an illness or accident on the way of life of the sufferer. Perhaps a simple example outside the chest illustrates this best. Two people require to have a foot amputated as a result of an accident. One is a ballet dancer. She is totally disabled by her accident and unable ever to continue with her chosen way of life. The other is an office clerk. After the initial treatment, he is able to return to work. It is even conceivable that he becomes more efficient because his accident ties him to his desk and makes it more difficult for him to chase around the office. Medically speaking each has exactly the same problem—yet one is disabled, and the other not.

A central issue determining disability is dependency. Some types of physical handicap make it inevitable that the disabled person has to rely on another for some of the simple necessities of life. For others dependency is relative. Those with determination will triumph over considerable odds. For others, a relatively minor handicap will render them helpless because they lack the motivation to fight it.

In relation to asthma the degree to which shortness of breath interferes with daily life will depend very much on social and psychological circumstances. A car will cope with the mobility problem but only for those who can afford it. The farm worker may well have to give up his job: the housewife will carry on, perhaps with help. The anxious and obsessional will cope less well with shortness of breath than the more phlegmatic. With asthma these problems only reach bothersome proportions in a few individuals with chronic and continuous symptoms. Besides this, there is the separate problem of the acute attack that introduces a different disability, that consequent upon unpredictable interference with daily routine.

Those that do become severely disabled have to resort to some help from the social services. A disabled car parking sticker or a car park voucher will make an important contribution. To become registered as disabled brings no financial help. Registration with the local authority under the sick and disabled persons act, qualifies the severe asthmatic for help in arranging holidays in special centres. Separate from this, the Department of Employment has a disabled persons' register. The services of the disablement resettlement officer become available to those on this register. The facilities are usually swamped by those with disabilities arising from accidents or conditions affecting the limbs and joints. The severe asthmatic would be theoretically eligible for these services and could be included in the percentage of disabled persons, firms are required to employ. In practice these considerations arise very rarely in the context of asthma.

The housewife whose asthma prevents her from carrying out normal household chores can apply for a non-contributory invalidity pension. This is a scheme to cover those who do not qualify for sickness or invalidity benefit because they have not enough national insurance contributions. Other benefits that might come within the scope of the severely disabled asthmatic are the mobility allowance and the attendance allowance. There are often charities that will provide help with specific aspects of management such as changing bedding, if this is advised on account of house dust mite allergy.

Air travel

Travel by air will only present problems to those with such severe and disabling asthma that oxygen levels in the blood are already low. A reduction in oxygen in the air in the aircraft cabin occurs at high altitude (a fall by about a quarter at 6000 feet). This could cause some embarrassment to the severe asthmatic and increase breathing difficulties: fortunately oxygen is readily available.

Self-help and some words of advice

Clothing

Few special rules need to be made about clothing, unless there is also eczema, when irritating fabrics, especially wool, will need to be avoided. Dust fragments which might break off fluffy clothing would irritate the asthmatic's bronchi. Detergents used in washing may cause skin allergies. The particular allergy which has cropped up in the manufacture of biological washing powders is unlikely ever to be a problem in the domestic setting, because quantities and concentrations will be so much lower. Keeping reasonably warm in cold weather is sensible, but there is no evidence that concentrating the warmth about the chest with woollen vests makes any difference to asthma.

Food and drink

'The food should be light and easy of digestion: ripe fruits baked, boiled, or roasted are very proper, but strong liquors of all kinds especially beer or ale are hurtful. If any supper be taken it should be very light.' This advice was given to asthmatics by John Wesley in his book Primitive Physick published in 1747. Though questions are often raised about diet by asthmatics, there are relatively few instances where specific adjustments make much difference. There are two general rules. First, large meals filling the stomach embarrass the breathing by pressing on the diaphragm. Secondly, every effort should be made to avoid being overweight. Excess weight has to be carried—and the lungs have to provide the oxygen for energy expenditure. So the overweight asthmatic will be relatively more disabled than the asthmatic who keeps slim.

Beyond these general considerations is the question of food allergy. Asthma is much more likely to be due to something that is inhaled into the lungs, rather than something swallowed. Yet the complaint that asthma follows soon after some particular food or drink is not uncommon.

In some instances a genuine, probably atopic, allergy is involved. The wheezing comes on within ten to fifteen minutes. Skin prick tests to the food or drink are positive. Foods that can do this are legion but common examples are cheeses, fish, nuts, and fruits. This asthma is rather more likely to be accompanied by allergic symptoms elsewhere—as might be expected when the allergen must be taken into the stomach and absorbed. There may be stomach upset—with nausea, sickness, cramping pains, or an explosive diarrhoea. There may be swelling of

153

the lips and tongue and the soft tissues of the mouth. There may be an itchy rash on the skin of the face, trunk, or limbs. All indicate that an allergen has been absorbed and distributed to all parts of the body. Food allergies can be manifested in one of these ways alone, or several features may appear together.

Once a food allergy is recognized it is easy enough to avoid. If a common ingredient seems implicated or several foods are involved then organizing an acceptable and nourishing diet might be a problem. If food allergies seem to be an important trigger factor, then the help of a dietician can be sought. At one stage, before the introduction of modern medicines for asthma, food allergies were thought by some physicians to be very important in asthma. Complicated elimination diets were devised to try to identify the offending food. Whilst such an exercise often brought about some temporary relief, the benefit seldom lasted long. The reasons are complex, but the conclusion must be drawn that in most asthmatics, food allergy, if it is important at all, is only one of several triggers. Eliminating the food allergen may help a little, but it will not influence the underlying tendency to asthma.

There are, however, other substances ingested in food and drink which are capable of triggering asthma by mechanisms that are not allergic. The best known of these is aspirin. This was mentioned in Chapter 3 in relation to the prostaglandins, that somewhat unusual group of substances which seem to be required throughout the body for a whole variety of reasons. Aspirin interferes with prostaglandin production and in a small proportion of asthmatics, perhaps about five per cent, this initiates wheezing. Very often these are young adults. They do not need to be atopic and may have had no previous asthma. They sometimes have blockage of the nose due to nasal polypi or may develop this later. The importance of identifying aspirin asthma is not so much in advising about the avoidance of aspirin itself—that is not difficult (though a careful perusal of the ingredients of some proprietry medicines reveals that it turns up in some unusual guises)—but rather in avoiding prepared foods that contain substances that, though not chemically related to aspirin, seem to act in the same way. Tartrazine and benzoic acid are important amongst these. Tartrazine is used as an artificial flavouring and benzoic acid as a yellow artificial colouring in prepared pastries, cakes, cordials, squashes, etc. The aspirin-sensitive asthmatic should avoid them all.

The aspirin story has a twist to its tail. The prostaglandins are many and the action of one is often opposite to the action of another. The balance of these opposing prostaglandins differs from person to person.

154

Self-help and some words of advice

Usually the balance in the lungs is such that aspirin has no effect on the function of the lungs. Not infrequently, as just described, it causes wheezing, but very occasionally it does the opposite; it relieves wheezing. Individual patients usually discover this for themselves. Aspirin certainly cannot be recommended as a treatment for asthma, but there is every hope that further research into the prostaglandin story will produce results that will benefit asthmatics in general.

There is yet another ingredient of certain foods and drinks that appears to initiate wheezing in a few asthmatics. This is the sulphur dioxide used as a preservative in preparing meats and certain drinks, especially synthetic orange drinks (which can also contain benzoic acid derivatives), and some wines. Alcoholic beverages feature all too frequently in the list of triggers for asthma. The alcohol itself is not at fault, but rather the additional components that give a drink its distinctive flavour. Whether the mechanism is allergic, chemical, or acts through influencing prostaglandins, is not known. Whatever it is, sensitivity to alcoholic drinks can be one of the more annoying features of asthma.

Smoking

For the asthmatic there is only one rule about smoking: don't! Irritability of the airways is a fundamental fault in asthma. To irritate them further with cigarette smoke is foolish. To continue smoking, so adding to the asthmatic airways' obstruction the damage and airways' narrowing due to the long term effects of smoking, is to court disaster.

Coping with coughing

Asthma is often accompanied by phlegm and coughing, especially as an attack is abating. The various techniques used by physiotherapists to help get up the phlegm, are much more applicable to patients with bronchitis than to those with asthma. They are essentially techniques that must be administered by someone else. When coughing, the asthmatic should guard against violent effort, for this not only compresses the airways, but can also set up reflex narrowing due to direct irritation.

The question of the use of antibiotics for wheezy bronchitis and for attacks of asthma which appear to be triggered by infection, is a difficult one. It is more important to ensure that bronchodilators are taken than it is to have an antibiotic. Furthermore most of the infective agents that trigger asthma are likely to be viruses which are unaffected

155

Self-help and some words of advice

by current antibiotics. Despite this, antibiotics are frequently pre-scribed and until a clearer understanding of the relationship between infection and asthma emerges, they will probably continue to be used.

It is easy for the asthmatic in an attack to become dry. Breathing through the open mouth is one reason for this: and often the shortness of breath prevents drinking. So, inhalations (as Dr Storr describes in the Introduction), can be helpful as well as soothing. It is probably the steam rather than anything else that helps, though some of the long established proprietary remedies such as Vick and Karvol deserve a more thorough scientific investigation.

Other points on treatment

Despite all that has been said about histamine as an agent producing airways' narrowing, antihistamine medicines which neutralize the effects of histamine, have proved very unrewarding in the treatment of asthma. They will often ease the incessant sneezing and running of the nost that characterize hayfever and other nasal allergies, but they rarely do any-thing for wheezing. Most antihistamines are mildly sedative. This pro-perty is sometimes made use of in treating the anxious asthmatic. In general however sedatives are not to be recommended. They can have a depressing effect on the parts of the brain which control the breathing muscles and, combined with exhaustion in a severe attack of asthma, this can be dangerous. Panic in an attack of asthma is more appropriately treated by the prompt administration of correct treatment for the wheezing given by a calm and reassuring doctor.

The other class of drugs that should be avoided by asthmatics is that known as the beta-blockers. These agents antagonize the effects of sym-pathetic stimulation on the heart and blood vessels and, as such, are widely used to lower the blood pressure and slow the heart rate. At the same time the bronchial muscle is caused to contract and so the airways narrow. Every effort has been made in recently introduced beta-blockers, to enhance the cardiac effects and minimize the bronchial effects. Though a considerable measure of success has been achieved in this direction, even the most cardio-selective beta-blockers must be used with great caution in asthmatics, and then only under close medical supervision.

Hypnosis

The state of hypnosis has been held responsible for the utterances of the Delphic oracle, mass hysteria, and the cure of asthma. Of the former two this may well be true; what of the latter?

156

Self-help and some words of advice

In objective terms, there is certainly a case to answer. The studies mentioned earlier (p. 69) in which inert salt solutions could be made to cause airways' narrowing or relaxation, certainly demonstrate that suggestion can influence the airways. It seems, also, that it can influence allergic responses. Under hypnosis, skin prick tests for atopic allergy were rendered negative in one arm, but not in the other, which it was suggested, would react normally.

A group of chest physicians based in London and headed by Dr Maher-Loughnan have been carrying out hypnosis treatment for many years. They use initially hypnosis by the physician, but try to teach autohypnosis as soon as possible. This means that the patient can hypnotize himself for fifteen to thirty minutes each day at home, the idea being to reinforce the therapeutic suggestions previously given by the doctor. Safeguards are built in against the fear of helplessness in alarming situations, against children demonstrating their skills at school, and against staying hypnotised for too long. During a year's observation the amount of asthma in a group of patients treated with hypnosis was reduced by one third. A control group given simple relaxation also improved greatly and not until eight months of treatment had been carried out did the hypnosis group fare better than the controls.

The questions that need answering about hypnosis are several. Does the recorded freedom from asthma go along with better lung function? If not, then is the apparent unawareness by the patient of the degree of asthma helpful or harmful? The shortness of breath experienced by the asthmatic can be very alarming; to reduce his awareness of this might well help him to cope more easily with everyday life. On the other hand, if it made him oblivious to a serious deterioration in his asthma, it would be potentially dangerous.

If long-term improvement can be substantiated it might well be questioned whether it is all worthwhile when seen in relation to the wide variety of pharmacological agents now available. A positive answer would perhaps only be given for the chronic asthmatic in whom the time and effort involved in organising hypnosis is to be set against the potential hazards of steroid therapy.

Psychotherapy

Any physician, by taking a careful history and listening sympathetically to an asthmatic patient's problems will be able to provide sufficient psychotherapy to alleviate much of the anxiety experienced by the average asthmatic. Misunderstanding is a potent source of anxiety in asthma as in other illnesses. A clear explanation of the mechanisms leading to episodes of asthma and the ways of most easily coping with attacks, are simple and important tools that any physician can use to help the asthmatic. A common sense approach to every day problems that are providing stress, perhaps with the help of a social worker, can deal with a vast majority of problems.

On a more specific plane it is important that a truly depressive illness be identified, for the appropriate treatment of this can lead to the asthma once more becoming manageable. Psychotherapy, as such, is reserved for the very few patients with complex psychological problems. Its design is usually the simple one of reducing anxiety and tension. It requires time and dedication on the parts of both the patient and the doctor, perhaps most of all in techniques which attempt to 'de-sensitise' the asthmatic to stressful circumstances. In the quiet atmosphere of the clinic, the psychotherapist suggests in a limited way the stressful psychological circumstances that are thought to be responsible for a patient's asthma. By applying relaxation techniques, the asthmatic can be made to accept a small degree of stress without becoming wheezy. Over weeks or months, the degree of stress is gradually increased and the relaxation reinforced until finally it should be possible for the asthmatic to experience without trouble a degree of stress in real life which had previously caused asthmatic wheezing.

Ionizers

Folklore teaches that the Sharav of the Holy Land and the Foehn of southern Germany are evil winds. They are hot and dry. They bring with them such malaise, that they are held responsible for everything from migraine to heart attacks, depression to car accidents. The physicists report that these winds—and others like them in other parts of the world—are loaded with positive ions.

Ions are minute atmospheric particles carrying an electrical charge either positive or negative. Normally there are very few of these in the atmosphere. They are produced by cosmic radiation. A few more arise with intense ultraviolet light from a scorching sun or after an electrical storm. In a closed room with little change of air, the ion content will drop to almost imperceptible levels.

Fascinating experiments have been carried out on plants and animals using highly-charged atmospheres. Both positive and negative ions seem to stimulate plant growth and hasten the hatching of silkworm eggs. Positively-charged ions slow down the production of mucus by the airways and cause the bronchial muscle to constrict. They make mice more susceptible to bacterial pneumonia and seem to place stress on the adrenal gland. Negative ions reverse these trends. At a chemical level it has been suggested that the positive ions raise the blood level of a powerful and versatile hormone, serotonin, that could certainly do many of the things proposed as a response to positive ionization.

Very wide-ranging claims are made for the effects of ions on man. Apart from the ill effects of the positively-charged evil winds, it is suggested that the lethargy that overpowers the average office worker towards the end of the day is due to lack of ions. A study in a Swiss bank claimed that by creating a negatively-charged atmosphere, workers not only became more efficient but that they also lost less time from work on account of respiratory illness.

How far can these claims be substantiated in respect of asthma? Sadly it seems not very far. Uncontrolled investigations often come up with substantial claims for success—but when a properly controlled trial is carried out these cannot be substantiated.

Acupuncture

The Chinese discovered the first bronchodilator, ephedrine, but it took 4000 years for the West to realize its worth. They also discovered acupuncture but the first serious analyses of its value have only recently been carried out. In asthma there is now good evidence that acupuncture can relax the airways. The effect seems immediate and shortlived, rather like that to be expected from a bronchodilator. Carefully controlled studies have unequivocally shown that needling of the 'Din Chuan' spot, just below the back of the neck, brings some relief to asthmatic wheezing, whereas the same procedure applied to non-specific points on the body has no effect. This observation could have important implications for research into the mechanisms of asthma. It could also form the basis for treatment in a few individuals, but the ease and simplicity of administration of a bronchodilator means that acupuncture will never be first line treatment for asthma.

Asthma Associations

In many chronic diseases, patients have found considerable mutual self benefit by meeting together, discussing difficulties with each other and sharing successes. Local doctors, nurses, social workers, and others often attend these meetings to explain aspects of the disease, answer questions, and stimulate interest. Fund raising is nearly always a feature of these groups and the money is channelled to some central advisory body to be allocated for educational or research purposes.

In relation to asthma, groups like this flourish in some parts of the world, notably in New Zealand. In Great Britain, the Asthma Research Council formed just over fifty years ago has concentrated its activities in raising funds for research. A move is now afoot to widen the horizon of interest in this group to embrace patient education and self-help. Branches of the Friends of the Asthma Research Council exist throughout the country and several of these are showing a growing concern with patient care as well as maintaining fund raising functions. If you wish to know more about the work of the Asthma Research Council the address to write to is: 12 Pembridge Square, London, W2 4EH. There may be in your area a local asthma association that performs a similar function; two of the best known are in Sheffield and Derby.

Index

acetylcholine, **41**, 44
acupuncture, **159**
ACTH, **123**, 128
adrenaline, **110–11**, 118
adrenocorticotropic hormone, **123**, 128
age of onset, 53, 64, 76–7, 79–87
air travel, 152
alcohol, 14, 155
allergy, **49–60**, *see also* atopy
   and childhood asthma, 81
   distinguished from infection, 62–3, 64
   and emotional stress, 69
   food, 153–4
   'immediate allergy', *see* atopy
   'late allergy', 57–60
      treatment, 124–30
   and occupational asthma, 94, 95, 124–30
Amesec, 121
aminophylline, 119, 138
antibodies, **51**, 59, 65, 89, 94, 103, 134
   IgE, 51, 59, 89, 94
   IgG, 59, 94
aspirin, 47–8, 154
Asthma Research Council, 160
atopy, **50–7**
   to animal tissues, 51, 52, 132
   and breast-feeding, 104
   in children, 81, 89
   to food, 153–4
   to household dust, 51, 56–7, 106, 131–2
   to moulds, 58–9
   and occupational asthma, 91, 94, 95, 98
   to pollen, 51, 52–5
Atropa belladona, see atropine
atropine, 64, 121–2, 135
attacks,
   description of, 31
   duration of, 28, 57

   management of, 12, 115, 116, 138, 148–9
   pattern of, 75–6, 91, 97
   premonitory symptoms of, 30–1
   time of day of, 30
   time of year of, 54, 58, 106
   triggering of, *see* triggering
Australia, incidence in, 101

beclomethasone, 126
Becotide, 129
benzoic acid, 154
beta-blockers, 156
betamethasone, 126
Bextasol, 129
breathing,
   difficulty in, 27–39, 49
   exercises, 146–8
   physiology of, 20–2
bronchi,
   description of, **22**
   narrowing of, 23–4, 59
bronchial irritability, 28–9, 32, 40–5
bronchitis, 25–6, 61–6
bronchodilators, 109–22
bronchospasm, **24**, 40, *see also* irritants
byssinosis, 96–8

'cardiac asthma', **25**
caring for asthmatics, 137–60
causes of asthma, 41–74
child–parent relationships, 15, 70–1, 72
children, asthma in, 79–83, 148–50
clothing, 153
congestion, 28
cotton industry, 96–8
coughing, 41, 59, 155–6

deaths from asthma, 6, 116–18, 142–3
defining asthma, 18–26

161

Index

162

Index